Advance Praise for Discover Your Wor

Discover Your Woman Within allows us to connect with the many different developmental aspects of ourselves. Becoming acquainted with archetypes in a practical and understandable way, we are guided to reflect and grow. Not so heavenly minded, it's no earthly good, Charlene's book is grounded in everyday life and escorts us to wholeness. —Patricia Clason, Coauthor of *Speaking of Success*

Charlene Tosi's wisdom and insight flow like honey onto the pages of *Discover Your Woman Within*. Written as a guidebook based on her women's workshops, it outlines the vital archetypes and stages of a woman's journey to her deepest feminine self. Through myth, story, dreams, imagery, and clear glimpses of her own path, Charlene leads the reader on a deeply experiential adventure of knowing the power of what lies within. —Djohariah Toor, MA, LMFT, Author of *The Road by the River: A Healing Journey for Women*

In a culture which teaches us to be obsessed with our external appearance, Charlene Tosi gently leads us down the winding staircase of exploration into the treasure trove beneath the surface of societal definitions. Through a rich examination of our bodies, archetypes, and emotions, we claim the power waiting to be unearthed and the creativity ready to erupt as we experience new rootedness in our psyches and world. —Carolyn Baker, PhD, Author of *Reclaiming the Dark Feminine: The Price of Desire*

We all need guides at different points in our lives to help us harness the best that life offer us or to move through challenging road blocks. With a mixture of wisdom, sensitivity, and vulnerability Charlene Tosi is that guide. In her book, she uses the power and magic of important female archetypes, to teach, support, honor, and stretch us. Charlene's words and stories about herself take us on a journey deep within ourselves. We finish the book stronger, clearer, and able to embrace more of ourselves than ever before. —Karen B. Kahn, EdD, Managing Partner at Threshold Advisors, LLC

Charlene Tosi has a remarkably clear understanding of women. Her years of experience working with women and her brilliant powers of observation have resulted in a book that can benefit men and women alike. Reading this book can assist women to blossom into their full womanhood by gaining a deeper understanding of the different parts of themselves.

Charlene's gift to men is to educate them about the inner workings of the female mind, to help them navigate what may seem like mysterious waters. This is bound to result in deeper intimacy and connection for couples. —Jim and Linda Brooks, Certified Facilitators of Couples Weekend and Shadow Work®

Charlene's book is a great gift to men. It welcomes us on a journey into the realm of feminine energies (archetypes), which has the power to make us more whole, more loving, and more open to the feminine wisdom that dwells within us.

As Charlene explores the personal meaning of nine archetypes, she shares her personal story, defeats, and victories in seeking to become healed of the diminishment that women experience in a culture that traditionally devalues the feminine. Her personal story brings her writing alive for the reader in a clear and compelling way.

There is deep wisdom in this book, which would take a lifetime to explore, but Charlene has a gift of making the wisdom accessible to us. She does this by pausing along the way to tell her personal story in a relevant manner and by providing exercises, which opens us to receive the gift of healing wisdom from the feminine. —Don Jones, Author of *Wisdom for the Journey*

For more than a generation, Charlene Tosi has inspired and facilitated the transformation of thousands of women (and hundreds of men) by teaching and showing them how to access their authentic, inner, feminine power. Now she has produced, with many moving personal expressions of her own journey, an easy-to-read guide that takes us all deeper, much deeper, into the marvelous and mysterious world of the Divine Feminine. She cuts through the sometimes complicated language of female archetypes and brings the landscape into clear focus with simple metaphors, personal stories and plain speaking. This book showed me the beautiful complexity of the feminine psyche.

Appearing on every page of this important book is Charlene's deep love, respect, and admiration for women everywhere. This book is for every woman interested in unfolding more of her deep, inner, and authentic self. Thankfully, it is also for those brave men who have, for too long, put off their own journeys of exploration into their inner feminine. Charlene's timing is perfect: this is the time for both. As I read her book, I found my appreciation for Charlene, for her work, and for the women in my life growing and deepening. —George Daranyi, Attorney, Poet, and Certified Leader of the New Warrior Training Adventure

To Linda Edwards,

May each step of
your journey reveal
joy of knowing your
Woman Within.

Best,
Charlene Tosi
September
2012

DISCOVER YOUR WOMAN WITHIN

A JOURNEY TO WHOLENESS

CHARLENE BELL TOSI

FOREWORD BY JUDITH DUERK
AUTHOR OF *CIRCLES OF STONES*

Discover Your Woman Within
A Journey to Wholeness

Copyright © 2012 by Charlene Bell Tosi

This publication is designed to provide information in regard to the subject matter covered. It is not intended to replace the services of a professional counselor.

Publisher: Tosi and Associates, Inc.

ISBN: 978-0-9859499-0-7

Project Development: Open Window Creations

Cover Design: Tony Scott Tosi

Interior Book Design: Greystroke Creative, Gary Hall

Editorial Services: Pam Suwinsky

A portion of the proceeds of this book will be donated to Woman Within International, a not-for-profit organization whose mission is to create educational opportunities for women to discover the power of who they are.

Printed in the United States of America

Copies of this book may be ordered from:

www.amazon.com

www.DiscoverYourWomanWithin.com

To my beautiful granddaughters Makenna Adelia Tosi and Aryana Belle Tosi. May you each continue to shine in your magnificence as you grow and discover the Woman Within you.

Your vision will become clear only when you look into your heart.
Who looks outside, dreams. Who looks inside, awakens.
—Carl Jung

Contents

Foreword

During the 1970s and '80s, when there was almost unrelenting pressure on women to pursue higher education, become professionally successful, and serve in community and volunteer positions, Charlene Tosi founded an organization that she quietly named "Woman Within." She sensed that with this continual societal pressure on women's outer growth and effort, they might need encouragement, even permission, to look within themselves. And she set about providing just that opportunity.

She spent the next decades of her life carefully structuring the organization, Woman Within, to foster that inner growth in thousands of women. The organization has served more than 15,000 women on four continents. In 1999, Woman Within International became a not-for-profit organization and is led by a board of directors. Charlene still leads weekends and has written a book about the fundamental elements that have nourished the women who have participated in the Woman Within Training.

Charlene's background had prepared her thoroughly for this work: education and employment in the healing arts, years of teaching young women in nursing schools and colleges, a serious commitment to understanding the feminine psyche from a Jungian perspective, and her own study at a Jung Institute, along with years of faithfully working with her own dreams.

But perhaps the element of her background that had most deeply prepared her for this new work was her knowledge of the pain of receiving very little encouragement or attention for her own inner growth as a girl and young woman in a rural household dominated by old masculine values.

In *Discover Your Woman Within*, Charlene Tosi writes of the course of a woman's life and the life events that serve as rites of passage ... the times most difficult, the issues most painful to bear, as well as the most meaningful and significant events. The main body of the book consists of chapters (2 through 10) on the nine Jungian archetypes she considers most important for women to be aware of: Queen, Infant, Child, Adolescent, Lover, Mother, Warrior, Shadow, and Crone.

Each chapter begins with a description of the archetype and how it functions in developing women's inner and outer lives. Following that are suggestions that help a woman recognize when that archetype is appropriately active in her life or when it needs to function more strongly or is being used excessively through her words and actions.

Charlene points out that an archetype can take over a woman's life without her being aware of how strongly it is influencing her behavior, thereby creating difficulty and strife for her. This is material that can be helpful to every woman! It will make each woman reading wish that all of the women around her were reading the book too.

The depth of Charlene's experience with these archetypes, along with her commitment and caring for women, come together beautifully in her meditations and affirmations. In them, she carefully guides a woman in forming a relationship with each archetype within herself, then speaking to it directly, asking for its help.

Judith Duerk, author of *Circle of Stones*

My Journey to Find
My Woman Within

*T*his book has been incubating inside me for more than twenty years. Perhaps it was even planted in my soul while I was in my mother's womb. My parents really wanted a son after having two beautiful daughters. My name was to be Charles, after my grandfather. Although my parents loved and accepted me, I felt their disappointment that I was a girl, and not the boy they wanted. I took this disappointment into my body and hated being a girl. As an adolescent, I wanted to cut off my budding breasts. Thus my journey into womanhood was fraught with feelings of disliking that I was female and never feeling good enough, which pervaded everything I attempted, even writing this book. Thanks to the encouragement and patience of my book coach, Patricia Lynn Reilly, I have stayed the journey.

My journey as a woman has been a lot like wandering in a dark and scary forest. I was never taught what it meant to be a woman. Even though I listened to other women—my mother, my sisters, my female teachers, my friends, who told me about menstruation and the possibility of pregnancy—being a woman was a mystery to me. Often I felt very lost, with occasional flickers of light shining through the trees showing me which path to take next.

As a child, I was sick more than I was well. I had rickets, numerous attacks of tonsillitis, and extreme bouts of all the childhood diseases—measles, mumps, chickenpox. I somehow knew that I needed healing and decided very young to be a nurse. I was intrigued by people's problems, and I wanted to find a way to help and heal myself and others. In the 1960s nursing was primarily a career for women, so I was connected mostly with women throughout my time at Vanderbilt University School of Nursing in Nashville, Tennessee. After graduating, I worked as a public health nurse for five years and as a professor of nursing for fifteen years. All of my colleagues were women and my students were women, with an occasional male student. I was surrounded by women, all the while unconsciously hating myself as a woman.

My Journey through College

When I was in college in Nashville, I struggled to fit in and find my way through the academic madness of completing a nursing degree. Fortunately for me, I found some guides who led me through this maze. After attending Belmont College for three years, I decided to transfer to the Diploma Nursing Program at the Baptist Hospital. The first guide was the director of the nursing program. When I interviewed with her, she looked at my file, picked up the phone, called the dean at Vanderbilt University, and said, "I have a student here for you and I am sending her over." She then looked at me and said, "You need to get a degree in nursing, not a diploma. That is the way through the forest that will serve you best."

I trusted this woman to guide me. The dean of nursing at Vanderbilt said, "You are accepted. We just don't have any rooms in the dorm for you." The forest got dark again—where would I stay?

I called my next guide, the dean of students at Belmont, and told her my dilemma. She offered me a position as a floor counselor until a dorm room opened up at Vanderbilt. She represented another clearing in my forest.

Being a nursing student was not easy. I flunked my first test in Fundamentals of Nursing. One of my professors of nursing came to my rescue and encouraged me to stay in nursing and guided me on how to take multiple choice tests.

My Journey through Relationships

Finding my way through the dense undergrowth of doubts, old childhood beliefs, and insecurity was a difficult task when dating and finding a life partner. Growing up in the hills of Kentucky gave me a very different social status than most of the students at Vanderbilt. I had never learned how to dance, never tasted alcohol or tobacco, so being on my own in the huge university with many different beliefs and styles of living, I felt lost, alone, and scared. Being thrust into the fraternity and sorority scene was overwhelming, and I wandered, trying to find who I was and what I wanted.

I wandered through many experiences with men to try to find a path that would work for me, and fortunately for me when I met Rich, the man I would marry, I knew in my heart that he was the one I wanted to be with for the rest of my life. My mother always told me to "save my body for the man I married," and that message had stuck in my head. I felt guilty even if a guy kissed me, and to have sex was way beyond my boundaries. I was often confused about how much to get physically involved and how much to "save my body." I chose not to stay a virgin and did not have any guides to help me deal with the guilt of having sex before marriage.

After my wedding day, learning how to be the perfect wife and still hold on to myself eluded me. I put all my energy into making my husband happy, which came across more like mothering him, and this behavior often drove him away. The forest was dark many days, and I often wondered what it meant to be a wife and a lover. I lost my sense of who I was as a woman.

My Journey through Parenting

Being a mother brought its own set of wanderings. My first child was born while we were in the military stationed far from our families, so no wise women were around to guide me through the maze of pregnancy and taking care of a baby. The tug of wanting to take the path of career and still be a mom tugged at me constantly. I loved being a mother, and I yearned to put my nursing skills into practice. The feminist movement confused me; the message I got was "Go out and get a job!" My heart wanted to stay home, and there was no guide to help me to find the answer.

Becoming a professor of nursing answered both calls, and again there was a clearing in my forest to find a way to fulfill my career and to be home on vacations, summers, and holidays. That was until I got emerged in getting my doctorate and lost sight of my family. Again I didn't have anyone to guide me. I spent several years in the darkness of my forest finding the balance of how to be there for my husband and my children and still satisfy my longing to share my professional gifts and my talents.

My Journey to Create the Woman Within Training
After my husband attended the dynamic program, Understanding Yourself and Others, led by Patricia Clason (now owner of Taking It Lightly), he cofounded the New Warrior Training for men (offered now through the ManKind Project) in 1984. As women witnessed the changes in the men who attended this program, they approached me, looking for a similar experience for women. At first I resisted because I was already working with women every day as a professor of nursing and was not even comfortable about who I was as a woman. However, the old adage, "You teach what you need to learn," became true for me. I truly wanted to know who I was as a woman and learn how to love myself.

Along with two other women, I designed a weekend patterned somewhat after the men's weekend. It became clear to me after leading four of these trainings that we did not understand women, and until I could tap into my own essence as a woman, I would never be able to teach or guide other women. Instead of learning by teaching, I discovered I needed to learn by going within. Because I was studying Jungian psychology, I chose to go into Jungian analysis. Through the brilliance of my analyst, Dr. Diane Martin, I learned how the images in my dreams symbolized different archetypal energies within me. For example, my dreams were filled with men dressed in black trying to break into my house. This symbolized my lack of Warrior archetypal energy that I had denied and put into Shadow. Dr. Martin helped me to see how I had cut off parts of my woman within and how those parts needed to be invited in for me to heal before I could help other women discover their lost parts of themselves.

During this time of going within, a friend asked me to once again offer a training for women. So we called together five other women to help design the now twenty-five-year-old program, Woman Within Training. After breakfast on the first day of our gathering, I went for a walk in the forest near where we were meeting and asked for guidance on how to proceed. In a millisecond a visualization of a castle with nine rooms came to me. The rooms symbolized the nine archetypal energies of women: Queen, Infant, Child, Adolescent, Lover, Mother, Warrior, Shadow, and Crone. The forest surrounded me with comfort, and the light shone through the trees like I have never seen before.

I went back to the group of women and invited them to close their eyes and participate in the visualization that had come to me in the forest. The women loved what I presented, and this metaphor became the catalyst for the rest of the program. The purpose of this metaphor is to lead a woman into her forest to find the sacred place where her woman within is waiting to be discovered. From this beginning the Woman Within Training was birthed and has touched the lives of thousands of women throughout the United States, Canada, Europe, Australia, and Europe.

All of the women who have attended these programs have been my teachers and my mirrors as I discovered my truth as a woman. I have laughed with women, cried with women, listened to women, held and been held by women, and have learned that all women hunger to be whole and embrace their magnificence.

It was through my journey of Jungian analysis and creating the Woman Within Training that I found the magic of archetypal energy and began to understand the necessity of the forest. Through my experience of working with thousands of women, it has become clear to me that all of us need guides, both internal and external, to find our path as we journey through our internal forests.

This book would not have been possible without the women who bravely shared their stories at the Women Within weekends. With the exception of the named contributors, the women discussed in the book are compilations; however, the essence of their stories remains true. Names have been changed for privacy.

Welcome to the Journey

We cannot say that the seed causes the growth, nor that the soil does.
We can say that the potentialities for growth lie within
the seed, in mysterious life forces, which,
when properly fostered, take on certain forms.
—M. C. Richards

SAN DIEGO, CALIFORNIA. Sixty women sit in two concentric circles in a room lit by one candle. It is dark. It is silent. Each woman listens to the whisperings of her soul. Each woman shares her feelings into the darkness.... "I am afraid of my own success." "I often am unsure of myself." "I am afraid of the depth of my feelings." "I don't trust women." "I was abused." "I feel so alone inside." "I feel unworthy of love and happiness." "I am angry at myself." "I am afraid of dying alone." "I am judgmental and critical of others." "I always feel rejected, unloved, and lost."

What brings these women together to share? Their deep desire is to be accepted as they are and to be seen and heard as women. They long to know the depths of their inner feminine. Thousands of women have sat in these circles at a Woman Within Training and have been seen, heard, and accepted as they are. Deep within every one of them is a desire to touch her magnificence and be celebrated as a woman.

By taking a sacred journey into the woman within you, you may discover hidden and unknown parts of yourself. To know the fullness of your potential as a woman is a gift to yourself. By stepping into your sacred place within, you can discover your potential, your strengths, and learn how to work with your limitations. In this book you have the opportunity to expand this knowledge of yourself and get unstuck from old patterns that may be blocking you from moving forward.

You are a magnificent woman who has everything you need to be successful and flourish in your life. Just as all seeds have built-in systems that guide and direct them to become what they are meant to become, you, also, have all the wisdom and capability in you to fulfill your true potential. There is no one else like you, and there never will be. You have within you powerful, invisible forces that influence what you do and how you feel. They are like "embryos" contained in seeds. Their growth depends on soil, climate, nutrients, care or neglect of the gardener, size and depth of the container. Your life is like a seed that contains all the potential of becoming a beautiful flower. When it is planted in the earthiness of the ground and watered, tended to and cared for, it becomes a beautiful plant. The wholeness and perfect balance of the nine Jungian female archetypes are contained within you. You are the gardener of your inner life. It is up to you to tend to the seeds of possibilities inside you so you can blossom into your wholeness as a woman.

The Meaning of Archetypes

I invite you to take a journey within to discover aspects of yourself that Carl Jung called "archetypes." In this book you will explore nine different aspects of yourself: Queen, Infant, Child, Adolescent, Lover, Mother, Warrior, Shadow, and Crone. Just as a seed grows from an embryo into a seedling, your body has evolved from generations of mutations and adaptations. Within you is an embryo that contains the foundation of your behaviors, your thinking, feeling, and human reactions. Your archetypes get activated by culture, hormones, family, people, and events. What gets activated is influenced by how you view everything that happens to you.

Archetypes are instinctual; just as birds build nests and migrate, so you have a magnetic pull to behave and evolve in a certain way. These are manifested in you as impulses and are guided by the unconscious. They can be identified by the way you think, feel, and interact with others. These impulses are also inherited from past generations and have their own initiative and specific energy. Thus, they can either interfere with what you want to accomplish in life or they can give deeper meaning to how you are living your life.

Perhaps you were taught ways of behaving that are against your natural instincts. For example, you may have learned that it is not okay to brag, however, it is important for you celebrate your accomplishments. Because you were told, "It is not nice to brag about yourself," that belief may still be present in disguised forms and acted out in unconscious ways, through subtle sarcastic comments or by putting down someone whom you perceive as successful, for example. Also, if a childhood trauma has been buried, the mind works very diligently to deny its existence. By unearthing the hurts of childhood, you can better understand how your behaviors helped you survive as a child; however, these same behaviors no longer work for you as an adult woman. When you realize these old patterns, you can change your behavior. When you become aware and understand the archetypes, you have choices and can balance them and step into your wholeness.

Imagine you own a magnificent dwelling where all parts of you reside. Inside the dwelling is a large banquet room with a round table. Around the table are the nine parts of you, along with your healthy, integrated whole self. You are in charge of these parts, and it is up to you to listen to each one and decide what part serves you in every situation. If one part takes over unconsciously, the result is disorder and imbalance. When several parts vie for your attention and want to be the center of your life, you will feel conflicted and ill at ease. All of your parts need to be heard and seen, and they each deserve a place at your banquet table. After they are each heard, it is up to you to make clear choices about which parts need to be activated in your life at different times. As you become conscious of the value of each part of yourself around your table, you have the tools to move through life with clarity and focus.

These archetypes are your inner experts, and each has a reason for serving you. Some of them may remain "offline" or asleep until you invite them into your consciousness. Other archetypes are overused and worn out and need your support and permission to rest and rejuvenate.

There is the potential for using too much or too little of the archetypal energy that is continually present within you. Archetypal energies pull inside of you from your unconscious. If you cannot name these energies, you may feel lost, confused, and discouraged. By knowing how to access and use your archetypal energies, you can adjust your behaviors and use the archetypes to serve you instead of being unconsciously controlled by them.

For example, if you have too much Lover archetypal energy, you may prostitute yourself. This means you give yourself away to others way beyond what is safe for your psychological development. On the other extreme, if you have too little Lover archetypal energy, you may close your heart down and keep your love locked up. If you have too much Mother archetypal energy, you mother everyone so that you can feel powerful and in control. Too little Mother archetypal energy shows up as being critical of others and yourself, keeping you from giving birth to new ideas and new relationships.

This book can serve as your map to understand yourself. By understanding how to use archetypes as a compass, you can navigate life in a new way. They point the way you need to walk to avoid havoc in your life. The more you deny feelings and behaviors driven by archetypal energies, the stronger they become. This neglect causes depression and for some women, the feeling of going insane.

By understanding, facing, identifying, and using the archetypes, they become your guides instead of your enemies. By trusting the knowledge and power of your inner archetypes, you find new ground to walk on; you are free to live a more creative, full life. As you discover and reclaim your wholeness, you have access to the magnificent inner powers and abilities to be all you have wanted to be.

Preparing for Your Journey

Welcome to the adventure of discovering your woman within. I wrote this book to enlighten and enrich your understanding of yourself. If you are one of the thousands of women who have attended the Woman Within Training, it is my hope that this book will deepen your experience.

I invite men to read this book to learn more about women and to discover aspects of your own inner feminine. By exploring these aspects, you will relate to women in a more open way and release negative feelings and misunderstandings. It is my hope that you will give this book to the significant women in your life.

At the beginning of each chapter, you will meet an archetype. I invite you to embrace each archetype and call upon her to journey with you through the book. You will explore the archetype's characteristics and explore what happens if a particular characteristic is overpowering you or is absent. There are many more archetypal characteristics than are listed here, and I encourage you to discover for yourself what they might be. Some of the characteristics are found in more than one archetype. I invite you to find the subtle way each archetype holds the energy in a different way.

At the end of each chapter you will have an opportunity to journal and practice exercises to assist you in discovering each archetype more fully. You will also find affirmations to support you. If you feel you are lacking a characteristic, or need to balance it in a more healthy way, take time to write the affirmations on cards and refer to them throughout your day. At close of each chapter, a Woman Within participant shares her experience of the chapter's archetype. You can learn more about each contributor at the back of the book.

In my imagination I have been talking to you for years, and I am thrilled that some of my thoughts are now in these pages for you to discover. It is my deepest hope that you will discover how magnificent you are and that you will step into your wholeness every day of your life. Come on—let's go and find that sacred place that holds all the wonder of who you are!

Chapter 1

Enter the Forest to Find Your Sacred Place

Your sacred space is where you can find yourself again and again.
—Joseph Campbell

*E*ntering the forest is the first step on our journey to discover our woman within. That first step, crossing the threshold into the unknown, is a symbolic letting go, a death of sorts to who we once were, in order to encounter the woman we are meant to be. Our true potential is hidden in the depths of the unknown landscape stretching out before us. The forest shimmers with both the light and the darkness, where the conscious, known parts of us play with the unconscious, shadow aspects of ourselves.

We all have times in our lives when we need to enter our forest. For some women this comes after a major event, like a divorce, loss of a friend or family member, birth of a child, loss of a job or beginning a new job, to name a few. Even when things are going well for us, we need to find that still, sacred place inside of us where we can deepen and enrich our lives. Going into the forest consciously gives us a chance to discover new paths through what otherwise may seem like a very dark and scary passage. Some women are hurled into their forests through episodes of depression and anxiety and wake up to find they are entangled in a place that feels hopeless.

These times require us to sit still and listen to what the forest has to say. Whether we enter the forest consciously or unconsciously doesn't matter. What does matter is that we spend time in the forest so we can find what is needed in our lives.

As we move into the forest we will find places of inner darkness in order to work through our doubts and fears. This is an opportunity to begin to understand who we are and to choose paths to our unique selves. Each of us has an inner myth based on what we believe about ourselves. These beliefs may be lies told to us by others that we have taken on as real. To break free of these falsehoods requires a journey away from who we think we are into the depths of "who we really are." During this journey, we will experience living our personal myths as we seek guidance from our dreams, imagination, and reflections and listen to the mysteries of the Earth.

As Joseph Campbell states, "If you follow a path made by someone else's footsteps, you go astray. Each of us has to find our own way." Don Jones, in his book *Wisdom for the Journey,* says, "When you come to a fork in the road, travel both ways in your imagination until you know which one belongs to you."

I invite you to choose a path in your forest and take a journey to discover your sacred place. There may not be a clearly marked path, and all you see is undergrowth and tangled vines. This may be an example of how your life feels right now, so realize that the way to your sacred place is through this seemingly impossible undergrowth. Know you have all the skills and wisdom you need to cut through the obstacles and make your own way. With each step the next step will reveal itself to you.

Take a few deep breathes and read the following visualization slowly, pausing at the questions to form images in your mind.

Imagine yourself in a forest. What does your forest look like? As you walk through your forest chose a path that feels right to you. After you have chosen a path through the forest, stroll down your path and wonder how your life will be different when you get to know yourself as a whole, complete, magnificent woman. After some time, your steps quicken as you begin to sense the possibility of discovering more about yourself. You know that the answers are inside you. You just need a place to explore and discover all your inner treasures.

Ahead in the fog you see the faint outline of a building. You can't quite see it, yet in your heart you know this is the place where you can discover and celebrate your wholeness as a woman. You take a deep breath and your steps become purposeful and steady. Your excitement heightens as you get closer and closer.

As you get closer you are see the most amazing architectural structure. It may be a cathedral, a palace, a mansion, a castle, a temple, a church, or some other magnificent configuration. Instead of a structure you may just see a clearing in the forest full of magical shadows and light. The image gets clearer the closer you get, and seeing it you know that this is your sacred place where you can discover your essence. What is your structure made of? What shape is it? How many windows, doors, and floors does it have? Does it have spires or turrets or towers? Is it round, square, or angular? Is there a wall or a moat around it? What color is your sacred place? What makes your place special and unique from any other place? Take all the time you need to see this place you have discovered in your forest. Imagine all the treasure and mysteries it holds for you to discover. Breathe deeply and take in the magnificence and beauty of this symbol that represents your sacred place and holds the wonder of your woman within.

This place is a symbol of a private, secure refuge. Symbolic thought opens the door to an immediate reality for us without weakening or invalidating it. The psychological mechanism that transforms energy is the *symbol,* according to Carl Jung. Symbols act as transformers. They transform energy in ways that better our lives and create new ways to behave in the world. Therefore, by accepting this symbol of who we are, we can transform our inner landscapes and how we walk through our lives.

Every symbol holds a treasure. Our sacred place is waiting for us so we can live a life of abundance that we deserve and not settle for less. Entering this place means we can be prosperous and have what we want and need in our life.

We can go to our sacred place any time we want to find answers to our questions and learn about ourselves. We can go there by getting a cup of tea and sitting down to write in our journal. We can close our eyes in the midst of a busy day at work and find ourselves in this place. Often when I am on a plane or riding on a train, I find this a perfect time to go to my sacred place and visit all those parts of me that are there to serve me. Even when there is chaos or a lot of activity around us, our sacred place is always there for us to enter. What is exciting about going here is we can visit any time, even every day! This is not a one-time journey. Every time we go there we gain new treasures and new insights. Each phase of our life, daily challenges, and upsetting experiences are all opportunities to return to our sacred place for answers, inspiration, and new knowledge.

In the past, we may have listened to others' answers about what we need and who we are. It is now time to go home to ourselves, to discover how expansive our inner life really is. In this book, we will explore different areas or rooms of our sacred place, so either a building or a natural setting will work. This place is found inside our mind and heart and is ours alone to explore.

Every area or room of this place holds a special gift for us to take forward into our life. Teresa of Ávila, a prominent Spanish mystic, Carmelite nun, and theologian of the contemplative life, sees our sacred place as a brilliant diamond-like crystal castle with many facets. The diamond that we seek is within us. What we want is what we are. We want to be valuable. We already are. We want to be rare and precious. We already are. We want to be shining and multifaceted. We already are.

This journey is about finding the treasure of our true selves. When we seek for our deep personal truths, we need courage and willingness not only to commit to take the journey, but to commit to live our purpose and our mission from a grounded, strong place inside ourselves. This journey not only transforms us, it transforms those around us.

The Sacred Place of Our Wholeness
By making this journey into our sacred place, we are making a choice to live fuller, happier lives and take responsibility for creating something more meaningful for ourselves. If we feel our lives are empty and we have nothing of value, we are in for a big surprise. Everything that we discover in our sacred place is a wondrous part of ourselves waiting for us to claim. Our journey to our sacred place will be uniquely ours and unlike anyone else's. We may have been trying to fit into a mold that someone else has prescribed for us. In

this journey, we are our only judge, and we can spread our wings and soar with joy and anticipation into our sacred place.

We may fear that if we discover an unknown part of ourselves we will be overwhelmed, depressed, or numb. This is like the Sleeping Beauty fairy tale when she went to explore all the rooms of her castle and found the forbidden spinning wheel. She did not know how to use it, so instead of going to get help to learn how to properly use this instrument, she tried to use it, pricked her finger, and fell asleep (became unconscious) for a long time.

Many of us have pricked our fingers on forbidden thoughts, and instead of searching for help and understanding, we put these thoughts into our unconscious. By understanding our woman within we can dispel the doubts, the pain, the discomfort, and the lack of knowledge of being a woman. For example, when I first purchased my computer, my iPod, and my iPhone, I used only a small part of their potential. I had no idea how to use and access all the functions and programs that were available to make my work easier and more fun. So, through trial and error and asking for help, I began to claim the power of the technology. Discovering our womanhood is like learning to use new technology. We have the keys and buttons. We have all the memory. We have the inner complexity and power to create who we are. Whether by reading this book or attending workshops or going to counseling, we can learn how to use the tools and power that are already within us.

Light emanates from our sacred place. Perhaps we may have been like Sleeping Beauty and are just now beginning to awaken to who and what we are. In the Jewish tradition, the Sabbath begins when women light candles at sundown to invite the light of Spirit into their homes. This light invites us to awaken to ourselves and accept and acknowledge our wholeness.

Getting to Know Our Archetypes

On this journey we will develop a new understanding of who we are. In addition, we will experience changes in our bodies and souls. Knowing our expansive possibilities will make us better lovers, mothers, career women, and givers of our gifts in the world. Our goal is to live our lives consciously and learn how to balance all our energies to support us.

To enter our sacred place we cross a bridge. This bridge takes us from the external world of our forest to our internal world of ourselves. When we cross this bridge, we leave the world as we know it and enter our archetypal world. This is our opportunity to explore the aspects of our personal archetypes. The bridge connects the unconscious with the conscious. By getting conscious of the different aspects of ourselves, we can then be in control of our lives and not be carried by the sea of unconscious behaviors.

Exercise

Find a place and time, ideally in nature, where you can sit in silence without interruption. Take some deep breaths and let your body relax as you continue to watch your breath flow in and out of your body. Prepare your body and soul to enter your sacred place. Let this silence feed you as you listen to the whisperings of your soul. Let this become a practice that you can return to again and again. This is about finding your still point, your center, and your readiness to enter into your wholeness.

The time is Now. Take that first step, and the way will open up before you. One step at a time, one breath at a time, continue your journey home to your woman within by entering your sacred place. With these words, enter the sacred place within your being. Choose one of the entrances, open the door, step across the threshold, and enter.

*I enter the sacred place at the center of my being
with fear and excitement.*

I take my next step toward my woman within.

*I am one with my sacred place. I hold its beauty
and shadows within me.*

I am full of treasure and mystery.

I welcome the adventure of exploring myself.

I embrace the expansiveness at the center of my being.

*I stand in awe of my potential and all that is waiting
to be revealed to me.*

My heart is open and ready to receive all of who I am.

Rhonda Gaughan's Story

I spent a large part of my life avoiding looking within myself. I was terrified that if I opened the door and looked within there would be nothing there. I worked really hard at controlling myself and controlling my life. I had the illusion that control would keep me safe. I also worked really hard to attempt to figure out what others wanted from me, so I could produce what was expected of me and then … I would be loved, accepted.

I lived with the impression that I had to work very hard to prove my worth. I had to justify my existence by doing enough. And consequently, I never felt I could do enough and as a result never felt enough.

Once I began the journey to look within—I have come to love and accept the many aspects of myself. Yes, the child part of me is terrified at times. She feels she is not enough. Not good enough. And she shows up at times when I am threatened or in fear of the unknown.

I have realized the more I can love and accept her, even in her vulnerability, the stronger I become. I was always afraid that if I appeared vulnerable—I would be hurt, killed, wounded. So at all cost I avoided getting in touch with my Inner Child. I have learned that my strength comes from my vulnerability. And I continue to work at fully accepting all parts of myself.

I used to have the impression of this huge vault door. Big, thick, heavy—locked. It was where I would keep my feelings and emotions hidden. Working on the perception that if I could only stay in control—control those around me—everything would be okay. As a result I totally lost touch with myself and my feelings. When I first began the journey of looking within I didn't even know what my feelings were. I didn't know how to identify what was going on for me. I had locked my feelings away for so long; I wasn't sure how to identify them and many times I was terrified to feel them. I have learned that the way out is through.

I now allow myself to feel—be with what is happening for me. Feel my feelings and get to the other side. I used to take the short cut. Pretend I wasn't feeling anything and get busy. I also was probably controlling someone or something. There is great power and strength in me to really see, feel, and be with what I am experiencing.

I grew up thinking I needed to discount, avoid my feelings. When I was twelve years old my brother was killed in an accident. He was fifteen years old. There was an unspoken rule within my family that said, "Don't talk about it." Still to this day, some forty-plus years later, my family does not speak about my brother's death. I have had an opportunity to speak about my brother's death, feel my feelings about this experience, and process my feelings. The feelings do not go away. Now I can be okay with experiencing my loss. I feel sad that there was no shared experience of this loss for all of my family. My commitment is to move fully and authentically forward into my life.

My mission in life is to teach, guide, and inspire full and free authentic self-expression. What I know is that I have to first be willing to go there myself. I hold a belief that I will not be able to take anyone else to that place within themselves if I am not willing to go there within myself.

One of the most powerful parts of being involved with others who are on the same journey is the unconditional love and acceptance I feel. I have struggled with loving and accepting myself, and I am connected in community with so many women who love and accept me for who I am. All of me.

I spent much of my life in forceful Warrior energy. I thought if I came at others with big fierce energy—they would not look beyond the surface and see the vulnerability within.

I have learned to be with that vulnerable part of me and no longer have to meet every experience with this force. I was pushing others away when what I really needed and wanted was to be connected. When I quit fearing my own connection to myself, I could allow others to be in connection with me.

My internal Mother within was at one time very critical and judgmental. I would internally beat myself up for ... oh so many things—you didn't do that right, why did you say that—what is wrong with you. I have come to more of a place of nurturing, loving, and supporting myself. There are times the child part of me shows up and I realized what she is looking for is to be kept safe, to know she is okay, to be loved and accepted for who she is. I stay connected to that part of me and love her through whatever comes up.

When I look at the issues I face in my life, I show much more love and compassion for myself. Life is my school for learning about myself and it takes practice. When I stay focused here—my life flows with grace and ease. I go into situations and new places with this intention—to flow with grace and ease. I release my resistance to learning and growing. I accept and go with the flow.

Chapter 2

Meet Your Queen

In every woman there is a Queen.
Speak to the Queen and the Queen will answer.
—Norwegian proverb

You almost have to step outside yourself and look at you
as if you were someone else you really care about
and really want to protect.
—Queen Latifah

*After you cross the bridge and enter your sacred place, take a deep
breath. Stand for a moment and take in the expansiveness. Find an
entrance that feels right for you. This may be a door, a gate, or an
opening in the clearing. As you enter, you are greeted by your Queen.
Look at her. She is you. She is the Queen who lives inside of you. Take a
deep breath and see yourself as a Queen. See and be seen by your Inner
Queen. She has been waiting for you to reclaim your magnificence. She
is always present for you to call upon when you want confidence, want
to step into your leader, be clear about your vision, be prosperous, or
bless others and be blessed.*

*I*n order for us to feel safe to learn about ourselves, we need to first recognize our internal guide who wants the best for us. This guide is our Inner Queen; she greets us as we begin our journey, and she will bless us when we finish our journey. By staying in touch with our Inner Queen who rules our domain, we reclaim our magnificence one archetype at a time, and we are willing to expand our understanding of how all the parts of us serve us.

When we were little girls, we felt royal and special. As I observe my granddaughters dress up in their princess dresses and crowns and sit on their toy thrones with grace and confidence, I am reminded that we enter life with Queen energy in our cells from the moment of birth.

My granddaughters also remind me of my childhood experience with Queen energy. As a child growing up in the Appalachian Mountains, I was neglected by my parents and used the mountains as my sanctuary to escape from the pain of being alone. My parents were too busy to notice that my clothes were stained and torn, that my hair was tangled and uncombed. Taking a bath once a week was a luxury.

And yet, in the midst of extreme poverty, I knew there was a Queen inside of me, and I made her into my imaginary friend. She lived on a mountain behind our house, and I called her Queen Ida to honor my grandmother, Ida Bell. I never knew my grandmother because she died when my dad was young; however, I was told she was a beautiful, elegant lady.

Every day on my long walk to school, I looked up at the mountain and saw Queen Ida smiling at me. She would then ride in a beautiful carriage down the mountain into the "holler" and bless me with strength and tell me how important and special I was. I buried the memory of this archetypal experience for forty-five years.

This chapter is about the archetypal Queen within us. This image has been destroyed, minimized, or even rejected by all the fairy-tale evil queens or the queens of popularity during our high school years. By embracing our archetypal Inner Queen, we expand our understanding beyond the superficial and damaging use of this archetype.

We all yearn to be special, cherished, and seen as regal and powerful. When we step into our Queen, we accept full responsibility of ruling all aspects of our domain. Our domain includes our inner life, our body, our relationships, our home, our workplace, and anywhere we find ourselves. Even when we are shopping at the grocery store, we are in our domain of planning healthy food for ourselves and our family. When we interact with others, we extend our domain to include every contact we make.

Stepping fully into Queen energy, we own our choices, talents, and responsibilities. We become the leaders of our own lives— no longer tossed to and fro by the expectations, responses, and fluctuating approval of others.

Characteristics of the Queen Archetype

Confident

Powerful Leader

Visionary

Prosperous and Expansive

Blessed and Blesses Others

The Queen Is Confident

The aspect of confidence is cultivated by listening to our inner authority, our Inner Queen. Many of us learned to distrust our inner authority; its voice was quieted by external authorities who claimed to know better than we did. We became experts at allowing others to lead us. Possibly we allowed the Inner Queen's voice to be drowned out by the voices of others, and we stopped listening to her altogether.

As we invite the Inner Queen out of hiding, we allow her to speak. We are able to discern between the messages we receive from society, religion, and other authority figures and those that emanate from our inner knowing, our inner authority. We are able to sort through the clutter of expectations and opinions to uncover the guidance we need and desire.

When we listen to ourselves we learn to know ourselves, what we want, and what is true for us. Marion Woodman in her book, *The Pregnant Virgin,* defines *virgin* as "a woman who is one within one's self and is motivated to follow *her* values and to do what is meaningful for *her*." This does not mean that we are alone and never listen to others' opinions and ideas. It means we value our thoughts, our wants and desires. To listen to our inner authority takes time, silence, and a willingness to go within. This can be done in many ways, such as meditation, taking walks along the ocean or through the forest, or writing in our journals. In the stillness we honor and listen to our Inner Queen so she can then inhabit our body and rule over our inner and outer domains.

In the ancient Sumerian myth, Inanna, Queen of the Upper World, lived as a slave to the people she ruled and listened to everyone else's expectations and directives. In her journey to the Underworld, she stripped off the masks, costumes, and scripts designed by others and learned to trust her own heart and voice. Inanna sacrificed the approval of others in order to find her authentic self. To become a balanced Queen, she needed to let go of her "old" self so she could ascend as a confident Queen.

Inspired by Queen Inanna, our Inner Queen invites us to release the conformity and false versions of ourselves to embrace our authentic selves, to speak with our empowered voices, and to begin to reign in all areas of our lives. When we can do this, we become visible to ourselves and others. We inhabit and appreciate our own strong and confident voice, stride, appearance, ideas, choices, and interactions.

Once we hear our inner voice and speak our truth with confidence, our body language reflects this change. We stand and walk with grace, and how we dress and communicate reflects our elegance. We meet everyone's eyes with our eyes. Others stop and take notice. They listen to our words that come from our hearts. By simply changing our body posture from looking down to standing tall, we allow our Inner Queen to enter our body.

When we are sure of ourselves and speak with confidence, others will trust us and feel safe in our presence.

Patricia is a stunning, tall, blonde college student who is searching for a direction in her life and wants to be authentic. She feels she has been a fake all her life and is full of self-doubt. She dresses and acts so others don't notice her. What she wants is to be fearless in her beauty and vulnerability. At a Woman Within Training she discovers her Inner Queen and invites this part of herself into her knowing.

Once she realizes she has a Queen inside of her, she looks in a mirror and gives herself the following blessing:

I bless my beauty. I bless my vulnerability, kindness, worthiness, compassion, passion, elegance, gracefulness, intelligence, wisdom, radiance, love, gentleness, laughter, fun and my willingness to believe the best in people.

She then looks herself in her eyes and says, "You are a Queen and you are where you need to be."

If a woman is overconfident, she acts as if her way is the only way. She is often described as an "ice queen" who has a false sense of power and believes that others are ineffective and that very few, if any, can meet her high standards. Others are afraid to approach her because of her cool demeanor. To cover her insecurity, she focuses on others' weaknesses instead of their strengths and goes to great lengths to magnify these weaknesses through idle gossip. Talking about others in this way gives her a false sense of power. She gloats in her ability to have a discerning eye for another's lack.

The weaker the ice queen feels inside, the more she talks and the less she listens. Those around her feel weak and invisible in her presence. She is so concerned about her own views that she does not realize that her behavior is intimidating and hurtful. Defensiveness is her armor that protects her vulnerability. The ice queen covers up her hurtful past by acting well-put-together and pseudo-confident.

If a woman is lacking confidence, she is silent and afraid to speak up and state her truth. She feels incompetent to be a queen and wants others to take care of her and tell her what she needs to do. She puts others on pedestals because she experiences them as more important than her. She capitulates to the requests, demands, expectations, and critiques of others, often at the expense of her own sanity, integrity, and well-being.

When I began to reclaim my Inner Queen, I realized how my dad's voice had silenced my inner voice. In order to reclaim my Queen, I needed to take my dad, a Baptist minister, off the pedestal. My dad's rules controlled my behavior and I was terrified to make my own way. I equated him to God, and it was not okay to disappoint him. So going against my dad's beliefs was like challenging God.

To escape the punishment of my dad and ultimately of God, I had silenced the voice of my Inner Queen, who knew what was important for me.

I was inspired by a very dynamic dream to once again listen to the voice of my Inner Queen. In the dream I am traveling through a dark tunnel, and at the end of the tunnel is my dad sitting on a very high pedestal shouting down at me. I take a huge hatchet and chop down the pedestal and watch my dad tumble to the ground. In this dream, I challenged patriarchy and God himself as I allowed my Inner Queen's voice to get stronger and louder and the voices of "Thou Shalt Not's" get softer and softer.

When women banish their Queens because of lack of confidence, they make it hard for other women to become queens. When we succeed, we may be criticized by others and begin to minimize, deny, or hide our success. Unlike the overconfident queen who will not listen to others, the invisible queen thinks no one wants to listen to her. The confident Queen knows when to listen and when to speak. She is aware of both her inner voice and the voices of others so that she can discern when to empower herself and others.

Affirmations for a Confident Queen

- I listen to the voice of my Inner Queen and I heed her guidance.
- I walk with grace and present myself as a Queen.
- I am authentic and connected to myself and others.

The Queen Is a Powerful Leader

The most important person for a Queen to lead is herself. To lead ourselves, we must know our strengths and limitations. When we know ourselves fully, we can then accept and love ourselves. When we accept and love ourselves, others blossom in our presence. They feel capable, productive, and motivated.

Being a leader requires us to serve others and ourselves to enhance and create the greatest good for all. There may be times when we need to let other queens lead, and it is through discernment from our Queen place that allows us to decide whether to step aside with respect or to step in with dignity.

Unlike when we are a child, when we can play at being a queen by putting on crowns and pretend we are being served by a court of ladies and lords, being a Queen carries responsibility and is sustained by the hard work of personal growth and discipline.

In some archetypal literature, it is thought that the archetype of Mother belongs to the Queen archetype. In my years of working with women, I have discovered that our Queen role is much broader than one of simply raising children. We are responsible for leading and guiding our children; however, we also are responsible to be co-leaders in our intimate relationships, our extended families, our workplaces, and our communities. Each decision and choice we make in our daily lives comes from the Queen within us who guides us in how we will serve ourselves, others, and the world. By doing this we maintain an energy of elegance and magnificence.

If a woman is obsessed with her power as a leader, she uses her power in manipulative, hurtful ways and becomes an ineffective leader. She believes she can do it all, and others feel intimidated and small in her presence. She dissects others by asking questions, demanding facts and details, accepting only logical answers, causing others to feel paralyzed in her presence. Goethe says, "We murder when we dissect."

Rachel, a brilliant woman, is president of her company and is thrilled to be stepping into her leader. Instead of using her leader to empower others, she barks orders and doesn't listen to what others need from her. This way of leading worked well for a while until her employees felt disempowered and began to resign one by one. Instead of replacing them, she decided to do their jobs, so eventually she was doing all the work for the entire company. What Rachel didn't realize was the toll this was taking on her body, relationships, and company. Because of the high stress of her job, she had little if any time for her relationship with her husband. She was overwhelmed and lonely. Her husband asked for a divorce, and her company was on the verge of bankruptcy.

It was at this point that Rachel decided to attend a Woman Within Training. When Rachel realized the toll her leadership style was taking on her body, her marriage, and her business, she was able to transform her understanding of leadership. She dove deep within and embraced the authentic qualities of her Inner Queen. She channeled the flow of her queenly power into listening and empowering others. After the training, she was able to rebuild her relationship with her husband, and the new employees she hired felt free to express their ideas and suggestions. They felt heard and supported.

The issue of power is not how to get rid of it; it is how to channel it. If a woman is a tyrant queen, she wants to do everything for everyone and is not aware of the far-reaching consequences of her behavior. She is ruled by the critical voice of her inner judge, and she demands perfection and suffocates vision in others. She is fueled by fear and is continually evaluating and comparing others to her construct of beliefs. The tyrant queen will do everything she can to destroy those who get in her way.

At the other end of the spectrum is a woman who does not know and accept her power. She puts on a cloak of invisibility so that others cannot see how powerless she feels. She is so afraid of her power that she suffocates herself by choking off her opinions and ideas and lets others rule her. Instead of speaking her truth, she sacrifices excellence and visibility to be safe.

A woman becomes invisible when she feels unworthy and believes that her needs are not as important as others. She may become a martyr, make unhealthy sacrifices, and manipulate and undermine the authority of others. If she does not access her Queen energy, she fails to think with logic, clarity, and discrimination, and she becomes irresponsible and depressed. Depression keeps women invisible queens because they feel powerless to be effective in the world.

Silence is the language of invisibility. Queens need to speak up and be heard. Others do not know where the invisible queen stands because she does not know who she is and does not state what she wants. Just as the tyrant queen sees the weakness of others, the invisible queen sees only her own weaknesses and magnifies them through her silence.

Affirmations for a Powerful Leader Queen

- I accept and love all parts of myself.
- I serve others from a place of connection with myself.
- I am a discerning Queen. I know when to speak up, when to stay quiet, and I am attuned to my own needs and the needs of others.
- I am a powerful leader, and my success does not take away from anyone else's success.

The Queen Is a Visionary

The Queen sees the big picture of her domain and communicates and manifests her vision in the world. As women, many of us were taught to think small and not to get a "big head" by telling others about our talents and our visions. The visionary Queen within us allows us to see and share our gifts as we communicate to others through our own inner seeing.

When women are disconnected from their visionary Queens they have no idea what to do with their lives. Yet they see others living lives they want to live. They have lost the vision of who they are meant to be. This confusion reminds me of the story of a condor raised as a goose. She spent her time on the ground pecking at seeds and occasionally flying with her fellow geese.

One day the grounded condor looked up and saw a magnificent bird in the sky, soaring high and gliding over the farms and farmland. "I wish I could be so large and graceful and soar so high." She didn't know she was a condor and that she had the same capacities as the magnificent bird in the sky. When the grounded condor realized she was looking at someone like herself, she stretched her wings and soared high into the sky. Women whom we admire, women we place on pedestals, and even women we sometimes belittle so we will feel better are modeling the visions of who we are.

When the visionary Queen rules our lives, we are inspired to move in new directions and get unstuck from the familiar and move forward with clarity. Our visions inspire us to change, to risk failure, to step beyond our boundaries. Our vision emerges from the compost of the difficult, the imperfect, the unacceptable, and the losses we have experienced, as well as the achievements, the happy times, and the successful moments of our life. Our vision comes from our heart—not our head.

When the Queen fails at something she sets out to do, she does not quit. Instead she learns the lesson from the failure, honors the lesson, and moves in a new direction or starts again. We are always planting new seeds of success through moments of seeming failure.

If we always have to win and cannot tolerate failure, we put ourselves in the bind of having to be perfect and expecting perfection from others. This may cause us to push others away when winning becomes all important to us.

It is sometimes easy to forget our vision and question our purpose in life. It also seems easier to be invisible than to risk getting hurt or making a mistake.

Linda, a mother of two young daughters, is a successful lawyer. She loves her family and her career, yet she feels pulled in many directions. She volunteers in her community, helps out her neighbors with babysitting, maintains an immaculate house, and longs for more balance and time to listen to herself. Through a practice of inner listening at a Woman Within Training, Linda stepped into her visionary Queen and made a list of how much time she gives to each part of her domain and reexamined her priorities. After listening to her Inner Queen, she rebalanced her priorities and now rules her domain in alignment with her vision rather than through obligation and resentment. She let go of things that did not serve her and gives more time to areas that nurture and sustain her. She balances her time and makes different choices.

If a woman is so focused on her own vision and ignores the dreams and visions of others in her domain, she is also an ineffective leader. She may be fueled by fear of failure and continually evaluate and compare herself to others. Perfection is her goal, and this blinds her to the expansive possibilities.

She trips herself up by focusing on the negative aspects of what she is doing or has done instead of looking at the big picture of her vision and all the positive aspects as well. I recently returned from leading two workshops in Europe. All thirty-two participants loved the training except for two women who were disappointed in the results. Instead of blessing what I did well and learning what I could do differently the next time, I spiraled into despair and told myself I would never lead again. As I hit myself over my head with my scepter, my visionary Queen reminded me of the many years the Woman Within program has been successful, with a long track record of inspiring thousands of women around the world. I did not fail to achieve what I set out to do—I just needed to readjust my lens. She reminds me to learn from the feedback from others and to remember that growth is in the balance—not in deflating or inflating my gifts.

The opposite of focusing only on our vision is refusing to do the work to discover our vision. Some of us may stay focused on the injured past, wishing for a fairy godmother (or knight in shining armor) to come along and transform us into beautiful Queens who will live happily ever after. Asking the question "Who will save me?" disempowers us. If we shirk the responsibility for our own lives, our lives will pass us by.

Instead of accepting the responsibility of creating and living our own personal vision, we stay stuck in the past and wallow in our wounds. The Inner Queen reminds us that in every moment, we're making a powerful choice—either we are taking full responsibility for our own lives and visions or we are capitulating responsibility while we wait for the fairy godmother to show up.

Affirmations for a Visionary Queen

- I am committed to my vision.
- I discern what is right and good for me and others.

- I use all experiences in my life to create and live my vision.
- I learn from my mistakes and failures.

The Queen Is Prosperous and Expansive
When the crown is placed on a queen's head during a coronation, she becomes a symbol of prosperity. She is handed a sword to symbolize her responsibility to guard and protect her domain and a scepter to symbolize her responsibility to bestow blessings on her people. Our prosperous Queen is waiting to crown us, to hand us our sword and our scepter.

Wearing a crown can become a great burden. Queen Elizabeth I said, "To be a [Queen] and to wear a crown is a thing more glorious to them that see it than it is pleasant to them that bear it." When Queen Elizabeth I was crowned the queen of England, the government was degenerate, the treasury was empty, and there was no military to protect the country, yet she led England into the Golden Age of Prosperity. She was willing to take on the responsibility of being a Queen, even when she felt powerless, her bank account was empty, and she did not know how to use her Inner Warrior to protect her country and herself.

Elizabeth I was referred to as the "Virgin Queen" because she didn't have a husband and also because she was complete unto herself. She stepped into the position of queen when others thought she was illegitimate, too young and inexperienced, and incapable without a man to guide her. She did not allow any of these naysayers to dissuade her from fully embracing the responsibility of being queen for forty-five years. In moments of heaviness and seeming defeat, remember that we are called to be in charge of our lives.

We are called to be the Queens of our own lives and domains for a lifetime. There is no time off from the task. Whatever the state of our domain, one step at a time, with the help of our Inner

Queen we can transform disarray into beauty, empty coffers into abundance, vulnerability into safety, weakness into strength, and despair into gladness.

One step to take is to reclaim our home and make it fit for a Queen. Sometimes I look around my house and compare it to others who elegantly decorate with antiques, original artwork, expensive furniture, and Oriental rugs. Then I look at my home through the eyes of my prosperous Queen and I see my walls with family pictures and celebrate the memories. I look at my thirty-year-old kitchen table and celebrate the many friends and family who have gathered here throughout the years. I am reminded that each item in my home reflects the story of a life well lived, and I realize how prosperous I am.

Our prosperity is not measured by what we possess, but how we feel inside when we inventory what we possess and the people we know. Our possessions and relationships are reflections of our souls, our lives, and our journeys.

In order to step into our prosperous Queens, we may need, as Queen Elizabeth I did, a council to advise us and guide us. Every Queen needs trusted, capable advisors to guide her in areas where she lacks expertise. If our finances are in disarray due to chronic spending and debt, we can find someone who understands finances to help us transform vagueness into clarity and debt into abundance. If we are lacking excellent health, we can seek out a wellness coach to assist us in achieving wellness. If our partnership domain is unstable due to chronic miscommunication and mistrust, we can find a therapist or attend a couples' weekend to transform mistrust and resentment into trust and gratitude.

All prosperity begins in the mind. As we interact with others we expand our sense of what is possible. This is a time when we can play with our magical Child in the infinite field of possibilities. We create prosperity by imagining what we want. What we believe is what we achieve.

Being prosperous is not just about having money. We are prosperous when we have friends who mean a lot to us. We are prosperous when we love what we are doing. We are prosperous when we give to others. In order to receive, it is important to give, save, and invest. Whatever we want for ourselves, we must desire for others.

When we step into our prosperous Queen, we understand the principle of flow. If we stop the flow by failing to receive, as well as failing to give, we become greedy queens. A fountain symbolizes the ability to circulate water to create a peaceful sound and reminds us that life is flow. If we turn off the fountain, the flow is stopped and it becomes a static fixture without movement and sound. So it is with the greedy queen. She may own many gifts and material possessions, yet she chooses to hoard these things and collapses in on herself instead of becoming the expansive Queen she is meant to be.

If we hold ourselves back from sharing our gifts, we unconsciously hold others back. Not only are we afraid of sharing our gifts, we want to demolish any other queen who is sharing gifts that are similar to ours.

Snow White's stepmother spent all her time primping and worrying in her quest to be the most beautiful in the land. She was jealous of Snow White's beauty and wanted her dead. She went to great lengths to trick Snow White into taking her deadly bait. Phyllis Chesler states in her book, *Woman's Inhumanity to Woman,* "A woman's ability to merge and affiliate with another woman can be used for good—or it can be part of a vampire scam." Through her research she has discovered that women unconsciously fear that an evil stepmother will emerge, and thus women have little trust of other women in the workplace. Kelly Valen surveyed 3,020 women about female relationships and published her results in *The Twisted Sisterhood*. Of the women surveyed, 84 percent said they suffered palpable emotional wounding at the hands of other females.

The greedy queen does not want other women to succeed, and she secretly hopes that others fail so that her success will be noticed. Marianne Williamson writes in her book *A Woman's Worth* that she receives more criticism for succeeding than she does for failing. She states, "It is clear to me that people in our society, at least unconsciously, hold the conviction that someone else's success limits their own chances."

At the other end of the spectrum is the pauper queen, who focuses on lack and scarcity. She is afraid there will never be enough, so instead of going out to expand her domain, she shrivels and hides in the dark corners. She panics easily about not having enough and worries about where the next dollar, experience, relationship is going to come from. She lives in fear and is unable to see her way out of her dilemma. When we get stuck in fear, we manifest scarcity. Fear and scarcity go hand in hand and keep us paralyzed.

In a Hebrew fable, a tearful beggar goes to a queen and asks for money. The queen gives him a small sum of money. The next day, a joyful beggar asks the queen for money and she gives him a large sum. What made the difference? The joyful beggar knew that not having money was a temporary moment in life and she was expecting to give and receive. The tearful beggar came from the "Poor me—I will never have enough" place and got little. How we approach life determines the reward we will receive. If we live in worry and focus on scarcity, we will not prosper. If we expect our needs to be met and live in gratitude and appreciate what we have, we will prosper and expand.

Both the greedy queen and the pauper queen live contracted lives focused on scarcity. One guards what she has, fearful there will be no more, and stops the flow of life's reciprocity. The other expects nothing, and this expectation is confirmed over and over again. They are both selfish. The greedy queen is so busy guarding what she has and sabotaging competitors that she has no inclination to give to others. The pauper queen is focused on scarcity and believes she has nothing to give.

Affirmations for a Prosperous and Expansive Queen

- I have everything I need to be prosperous.
- I am open to receiving abundance.
- I give to others freely.
- I am visible, successful, and celebrate success in myself and others.

The Queen Is Blessed and Blesses Others

True blessings originate with the creator, as portrayed in the story of Genesis. Everything that was made was blessed to be fruitful and multiply. Today, we throw around the concept of blessing nonchalantly by saying "Bless you" when someone sneezes or we sign our letters or e-mails with the word "Blessings." We say blessings before our meals, and we say we are blessed. Part of being a Queen is the ability to bless others, yet few of us have been taught how to do that or what the act of blessing means.

Although the word *blessing* is often tied to a religious belief, for the purposes of the archetypal Queen, the definition I propose is to "confer prosperity onto another." Gary Smalley and John

Trent in their book *The Blessing* outline the importance of parents blessing their children as well as others in our lives. They outline the five aspects of blessing to be meaningful touch, spoken blessing, attachment of high value to the other, picturing for the other a special future, and active commitment to the other to help him or her realize that future. When we consider the depth of this kind of blessing, we can see the responsibility such a blessing carries.

Robert Moore and Douglas Gillette, authors of *King, Warrior, Lover and Magician,* believe that before we can bless others, we must first be blessed by our mother and father. Receiving our parents' blessings heals our Inner Child's wounds so that we can fully step into our Queen energy.

When my dad was dying from the complications of Parkinson's disease, he was hospitalized with pneumonia. He had lost his ability to speak in words that could be understood; however, he was very cognizant of others speaking to him. Even if I couldn't understand him, I wanted him to bless me and I wanted to thank my dad for giving me life. When I entered his hospital room, he was sitting in a chair dressed in a burgundy robe, looking like a king. When I asked him to bless me, he opened his arms and invited me to crawl into his lap. I laid my head on his shoulder and he put his weak, trembling arms around me. I felt the strength of his Inner King, and my body took in his blessing from the tip of my head nestled into his neck to my toes, resting on his bony shins. I sobbed and my body shook with grief and joy. I thanked and blessed my dad for how he had guided and taught me through the years.

After my father passed, several years later on one of my visits to Kentucky, my mother said she had something important to say to me. My heart leapt in my chest, and I thought, *Oh, no, what have I done wrong!* (A typical child response!) We sat across from each other at the kitchen table, held hands, and looked in each other's eyes. My mother, with tears in her eyes, said, "Charlene, I know I wasn't always the best mother, and I really want you to forgive me for that. I didn't know how to be a mother and I did the best I could because I wanted the best for you. I don't really understand what you are doing with all your workshops, and I want to bless you in your work, because I know it is God's work." Both of us were crying as we held each other, forgave and blessed each other. Now, Alzheimer's has taken over my mother's mind, yet her blessing will be in my heart forever as I carry it forth to men and women in my life—and most of all—into my heart as I offer her blessings to myself.

It is never too late to get a blessing from our parents. If our parents are living, we can ask them to bless us. One way to do that is to ask them to tell us what they appreciate about us and what they wish for us in the future. We can even write out what we want them to say and have them read it to us.

If this isn't possible or our parents are not alive, we can ask some trusted friends to role-play as our caregivers. We can then write out the blessing we want to hear from our parents and ask our friends to read it to us. As we listen to these words we can close our eyes and visualize our parents saying these words to us.

After we have been blessed by our parents, we are ready to bless others. When we bless others, we feel deep value and care for them and we truly want them to receive all the abundance that they deserve. Instead of making up a blessing, we can first ask what they want to have happen in their future. We then tune in to this person's desire and place our hand on her head or heart (with her permission) and visualize her manifesting her dream. Part of blessing another is our commitment to help this person achieve her dream through encouragement and regularly visualizing her being successful.

The Inner Queen asks for blessings from others whom we trust.

Let others know what we need to hear and take in their blessing to feed our Inner Queens as we continue to serve and bless ourselves and others.

Affirmations for a Blessing Queen

- I am blessed by both my parents.
- I bless others and see them as prosperous and expansive.
- I ask for blessings from those I trust.
- I bless myself daily.

Questions and Exercises to Discover Your Queen Archetype
Take some time to listen to the voice of your Inner Queen. Focus on the image of your Queen and ask her for guidance to find out what is true for you.

Look at yourself in the mirror and say, "I am a radiant, confident Queen." Dress and stand in a way that projects confidence.

Find people in your life who exemplify the qualities of grace, confidence, competence, and prosperity. Spend time around them to learn how they incorporate these attributes into their life.

How does your home reflect your Queen? What are some things you can do to make your home fit for the Queen you are? Take time to assess and rearrange your home to reflect your magnificence.

Form a council of support around you. Make a list of people in your life whom you can call on to serve as your council in specific areas of your life.

Ask your parents for a blessing. You may want to write down what you want to hear from your parents and ask them to read it to you.

If your parents are no longer living, write down what you want to hear from them and have a friend or therapist read this blessing to you.

List examples of your life when you have felt most queenlike, or when you wished you could have acted more like a queen.

Monica Robinson's Story
My Queen archetype has emerged more evidently in recent years. As my life has become increasingly determined by outer forces— navigating conflicting job roles, juggling multiple jobs, and tending to my own well-being in the midst of often incompatible demands, the Queen has been crucial in holding an effective stance. Prior to her conscious appearance, emotions, reactivity, feelings of being overwhelmed, and difficulty holding boundaries or reasonable prioritization tended to rule.

I draw on the Queen to listen with an unbiased ear, to speak hard things diplomatically, and to stand by what I think is right or fair or necessary. She refocuses me on the days when I question why I'm doing what I am doing, and she reminds me of my purpose and greater intention when my work feels pointless, ineffective, or unappreciated. My Queen takes a pause to evaluate whether or not I should take on another task or responsibility and can step into a flurry of activity and ask what is most important at this moment. She monitors what challenges my sense of integrity and asserts where my values lie.

My Queen expresses her love and concern for clients, friends, and the world at large through her blessings outwardly expressed or held in quiet intention. In conjunction with my Crone, the Queen is connected to a spiritual framework and is essential in forging the peace that comes from efforts toward clarity, appreciation of difficult paths, and an unquestioning knowledge of the value of my perspective. As I deepen in awareness of myself and others, my Queen is more present, more active, and has greater power to hold all of me in balance.

Chapter 3

Hold Your Infant Self during New Beginnings

An empty book is like an infant's soul, in which anything may be
written. It is capable of all things, but containeth nothing.
I have a mind to fill this with profitable wonders.
—Thomas Traherne

There is something helpless, weak, and innocent—
something like an infant—deep inside us that suffers
in ways we would never permit an insect to suffer.
—Jack Henry Abbott

*As you walk about in your sacred place, you discover an area dedicated
to new beginnings, perhaps a nursery where an infant sleeps or a
nursery where seeds are planted and brilliant green shoots are popping
up through the earth. Each day starts in this place of possibilities—the
room of new beginnings. This is where the sun rises every day to bring
in the newness of beginning again. Breathe in what it is like to witness
the pure goodness of life and the innocence, helplessness, and trust of the
Infant archetype.*

*A*ll of our life experiences begin in this room of new beginnings. When we start a family, a new relationship, move to a new city, begin a new career, become ill, or go back to school, our Infant archetype is activated. When a woman is pregnant with her first child, starting a new business, planting a garden, or writing her first book, she accesses her Infant archetypal energy. It is during these times that we need to listen to our Inner Infant and surround ourselves with supportive people who can celebrate and support us.

Spring reminds us of the newness of life as the Earth cycles every year to keep us in touch with our Infant archetype. Just as a little baby, a new day, or a tender sprout is filled with innocence and purity, so is each new moment of our life. Our Infant archetype takes these moments and transforms them to create the essence of who we are today.

Characteristics of the Infant Archetype

Pure Goodness

Helpless and Dependent

Innocent

Trusting

The Infant Is Pure Goodness
The Infant archetype reminds us that pure goodness is at the core of who we are. We were born to bring our special gifts and talents to bless and heal the world. We are each unique; there will never be another just like us. When we love and accept the purity and uniqueness of our Inner Infant, we accept our golden potential to launch into anything new.

Carl Jung refers to this archetype characteristic as the "Divine Child," which is the part of us that holds the promise of a future filled with joy and peace. This pure goodness is the all-powerful center of the universe, and every human being is born with a spark of divinity. When we accept our pure goodness or our divinity, we can turn to our internal source and know that we are on the right path. This source of life is magical and empowering, and holds our enthusiasm and excitement.

When we look in a newborn infant's eyes, or watch flowers burst forth from the Earth, we are reminded of this pure goodness. Every birth of something new brings a promise of hope. This quality keeps us feeling fresh and wholesome when we accept the godlike nature of our being. Remembering that the Infant is our connection to Source, whether named God, Goddess, Higher Power, or any other belief that keeps our intention and purpose pure. To move through new experiences we need to remember our connection to Source.

When we were in our mother's womb we got messages from her that affect how we show up in the world as adults. Some of these messages may continue to sabotage our new endeavors. If our mother was unusually tense, so may we be. If she was sick a lot, so may we be. If she was eagerly anticipating a boy and we were born a girl, we might feel unworthy and unwanted. If she desperately wanted us and made many attempts to get pregnant, we might grow up feeling like we are better than others.

Our pure goodness is often covered up and dimmed by how we were treated as an infant. If we were worshiped and adored and seen as a toy or prize as an infant, we grow to expect everyone to treat us the same way. We may feel entitled to be praised and loved and become Queen Babies as adults. This happens when our parents are unable to gently take us down from our high chair and help us to plant our feet on the solid ground of reality. We expect others to give us everything we want immediately, without having to ask. When too much Infant energy takes over a project or a relationship, we stomp our feet and cry louder to get what we want. Instead of manifesting our goodness, we drive others away and get caught in the illusion that we can do no wrong.

At the other extreme, if we were ignored and unloved as an infant, we focus on our lack and our limitations in new situations. For example, in new situations, we may feel useless, and we forget our connection to our pure goodness and carry a sense of worthlessness and shame into everything we do.

For me, the first sentence I heard at my birth was, "Oh, no, not another girl!" I was the third daughter born to parents who wanted a boy to carry on the family name. My name was supposed to be Charles and was changed to Charlene. From that moment on, my being was infused with messages: "You are a disappointment." "You are not good enough as you are." "Boys are needed to keep the family name going and you can't do that!" These messages drove me to work hard to be good enough. I wanted to prove that I was special, and my tendency was to give up trying. I needed to consciously change these messages so I could stop sabotaging my new beginnings. So, now I reassure my Infant self that she is good enough. I take time to see and acknowledge my pure goodness.

When we are in the infant stage of a relationship, a project, or an idea, forgetting that we are good corrupts and sabotages our progress. Sometimes it benefits us to remember that we have a divine spark alive in us. We all have a diamond within us that contains all the facets, the sparkle, the beauty, and the purity of who we are. As adults it is up to us to polish the diamond of who we are and treasure our value.

Affirmations for an Infant of Pure Goodness

- All of my new experiences are pure and full of unique possibilities.
- I am a good person.
- I am whole.
- I am loved and lovable just as I am.

The Infant Is Helpless and Dependent

When we start a new job, attend a new school, look for a new place to live, move to a new city, are a patient in the hospital, or start a new relationship, we activate the helpless and dependent part of the Infant archetype. Just as a newborn baby is helpless and dependent on others to serve her and meet her needs, so do we feel a similar helpless, dependent feeling in new situations. By being aware of this feeling, we can take action that will serve our newness. If we ignore this characteristic, we may be overcome with too much information and feel even more helpless.

In addition, when a new situation is scary or traumatic, like the loss of a job or relationship, the infant part of us will cry out to be heard. It is important to take the time to listen to our infant's needs because it is in the space between the death of the old and the birth of the new that a million possibilities exist. Just as an infant at the moment of conception has millions of chromosomes that decide her makeup, so does the new moment hold pregnant possibilities for us.

The infant expresses her needs and wants through sounds and experiences life through her senses. As Josephine Klein says in *Our Need for Others and Its Roots in Infancy*, "The self is like a stream that needs a container to adjust from being a water creature to being a dweller on dry land. The mother is the infant's psychological skin." We learn how to care for ourselves and others based on how we were cared for. Body-centered sensations are a part of the primitive self, and the infant part of us needs others to understand what we need in a new situation.

As adult women, when we act helpless in order to get others to take care of us or to feel sorry for us, we are overcome by too much helpless Infant energy and stay stuck there instead of asking others for guidance. We cling to those we perceive as authority figures. For example, many women become helpless around finances and rely on their partners to make all the financial decisions.

Many years ago my husband, along with many of his coworkers, invested a large amount of money in a recording company. I went with my husband to listen to the sales pitch, and my Inner Infant was screaming that this salesman was not trustworthy. My neck was beet red, my heart was pounding, and my hands were sweating. All the sensations in my body were telling me that this was not a good thing to do. Instead of honoring the signals of my body, I succumbed to the helplessness of the moment and went along with the investment, only to be visited by the IRS in a few short months to let us know this investment was fraudulent and we had to return all the money to the government. Instead of consulting my inner guide—which at that moment was my Infant archetype—I stayed helpless and silenced my screaming infant.

An example when I listened to and used my helpless Infant archetypal energy was when we sold our first house. I felt helpless and dependent because selling a house was a brand new experience for me. We had to rely on the knowledge and expertise of a real estate agent. As we worked with this agent, my body became very uncomfortable with her pricing. She priced our house very low so she could sell it fast and get the commission. She was taking advantage of our newness and helplessness. The Infant inside me was screaming to find another agent, and this time I listened to her! My Infant knew our house was worth more, so I listened to her. We obtained another agent and sold our house for thousands more than the first agent had priced it. When our adult self does not listen to our helpless Infant's wisdom, we neglect our needs and wants and rob ourselves of an authentic experience.

When we feel lost and little inside, yet act self-sufficient, we abandon our Infant inside us. We are unwilling to be helped and supported. The mantra in our head is "I can do it all by myself," which creates burnout and overwhelm.

Take Linda, for example. She is a full-time physical therapist who works 50 to 60 hours a week to compensate for others who need time off. She has three small children at home and her husband is physically disabled and not able to help her out with dinner or the kids because he cannot drive. Linda is completely overwhelmed and exhausted and cannot seem to grasp that it is her right and responsibility to ask for help. She complains about what her work is doing to her, how helpless her husband is, and cannot see that it is her responsibility to find a way to work less and get support from others. Inside she feels totally helpless, and yet on the outside she looks very strong.

At a Woman Within Training, Linda shared her story and felt the burden of all the responsibilities she has taken on. By participating in an exercise through which she experienced the love and support of other women and accepted her helpless Inner Infant, she emerged ready to ask for help and support in rearranging her life in a new way.

If our helpless, dependent Infant is not acknowledged, we become fragmented and anxious. Our distress becomes intolerable and the Infant inside of us cries and cries and goes unheard.

Affirmations for a Helpless and Dependent Infant

- I accept my body sensations as important messages for me.
- I nurture and protect my Inner Infant.
- I am open to relying on others for help in new situations.

The Infant Is Innocent

An infant is like a blank slate, vulnerable and easily filled with others' projections, expectations, and dreams. Imagine you have a blank piece of paper in front of you that holds all the good you deserve. The paper is innocent. It is simply blank. You are the one to fill up the page with pictures or words in color or in black and white. Our Infant archetype wants us to realize our innocence and purity and calls to us to fill up the blank pages of our life with enriching experiences. As we begin each day we have a blank page to fill.

A newborn infant's eyes reflect freshness, simplicity, and connection to the sacred. A tiny green sprout pushing through the rich earth is vulnerable and strong. This innocence is directly related to the soul of who we are. The infant's mind is like a vast new world: unexplored, unknown, and with no meanings attached. She has only her instinctual drives—crying, smiling, sleeping—to fulfill her needs and feel good. A tender sprout is determined to become a beautiful flower.

The Infant archetype is receptive and eager to learn all that life has to teach. Every experience, whether painful or pleasurable, leaves its mark on the infant's brain. The infant reflects and responds through the process of mirroring, where the (m)other reflects back positive aspects of the infant.

Our parents imprinted their behaviors and attitudes on this innocent part of us. All of their touch and feeling tones registered in our bodies and began to shape our choices and behaviors. Deep inside, we knew we were perfect; however, our parents had the power to override and mask our wonder-full-ness. Our innocent soul contains our seeds of greatness that need the love and connection of our caregivers so we can develop our potential. All of us have a yearning to return to the time and place where we feel loved and are well taken care of.

When starting something new, we need mirrors—others who can help us hold the thoughts and experiences of our new experiences. This is where a coach, a therapist, or a trusted friend can be very helpful to reflect back our experience and affirm our validity and worth.

If we stay stuck in the innocent characteristic of the Infant archetype, a couple of things can happen. First, we stay an open book and wear our feelings on our sleeves. All the feelings and reactions of others get stuck to our Infant self, and we lose our identity as we shape and conform to others' expectations. The result is a false self that destroys us and wears us down through the constant need to shape-shift and become what others need or want.

Second, because acting innocent is cute and adorable, we can get into dangerous situations in which we may be taken advantage of. As a twenty-year-old college student, I often stopped by an art gallery on my way to class. The artist was an intriguing gentleman around fifty years old, and he asked if he could paint nude pictures of me. As an attractive young woman, I flirted with him from a very innocent place. Because I was overprotected growing up, I was not exposed to or taught about the potential dangers in the world, and I was naïve. In my innocence, I was receptive and felt flattered that he saw me as a woman instead of a child, and I yearned to be "seen." Since my father rarely saw and affirmed me, I yearned to be seen by a man who could be my surrogate father. What better way to be adored than to be nude as someone put an image of me on his blank page? However, my stomach began to churn, and I began to see the potential danger of being exposed and possibly taken advantage of sexually. I said no and stopped visiting this art gallery. The struggle for me was how to nourish and embrace my innocence without getting into dangerous situations.

Often we allow others to write their insecurities, anger, and fear on *our* blank page. As the page gets fuller, we get more anxious, insecure, angry, and less trusting of others. We allow others' judgments to take over instead of being in charge of what goes on our page. Being innocent and wanting to be there as a blank page for others throws us out of balance as we take on others' projections and lose ourselves. Recognizing that we are in charge of our innocence, instead of our innocence being in charge of us, frees us up to express and feel the gifts of innocence.

When we ignore the innocence of the Infant, we fail to thrive in our newness. If we deny our innocence, we become hardened to learning new things and are not receptive to the ideas of others. We settle for the status quo because we are afraid to imagine new possibilities.

To cultivate our innocence we need to practice seeing things as if we had never seen them before. In the Buddhist tradition this is called the "beginner's mind." For example, we can take time to really *see* each sunset from an innocent, new place, as if we have never seen one before. We can be acutely aware of the odors, the sounds, the feeling of air on our skin, and the colors as they change and deepen. Taking this perspective by looking at a flower, an animal, our best friend, our partner, or an infant deepens our sense of newness and enriches our lives. Innocence is about experiencing life with all our senses and discovering a new depth of ourselves.

Affirmations for an Innocent Infant

- I am in charge of what gets written on my blank page of each new day.

- I am aware of my body sensations and use them to give me information about my new experiences.

- I am receptive and eager to learn from all that life has to offer.

The Infant Is Trusting

We form our template of trust when we are in our mother's womb and continue to shape it in the first two years of our life. Infant girls learn early to connect and read faces. In comparison to a boy's brain, a girl's brain has a larger communication center, bigger emotional center, and greater ability to read cues in people. In Louann Brizendine's book, *The Female Brain,* the author describes how estrogen is secreted in massive amounts from ages 6–24 months in infant girls. This enhances the brain circuits for observation, communication, tending, and caring. If young girls are placed in stressful situations at this early age, their nervous systems are imprinted and as adults they have a harder time trusting others.

Trust for an infant girl is developed when she receives consistent, reasonable, predictable, respectful, and loving care. If these are not available, she will begin to build defense mechanisms and take on masks to protect her vulnerable self.

The infant knows her body and trusts her body to give her signals for what she needs. By listening to our Infant archetype, we can lead a healthier life. The Infant archetype will tell us when we are hungry, when we need to rest, when we are threatened, or when we need to scream.

If we cling to authority figures instead of trusting our own instincts and capabilities, we become more and more helpless and stay stuck in our infant behavior. Authority figures can range from bosses to partners to friends and even to our own children. When we are exhibiting too much infant trust, everyone thinks they know what we need better than we do. Therefore, because our ideas are so fragile and new, others suggestions tend to step on and crush our beginning moments. In the infant stage of development, it is easy for all the energy to be sapped out by too much dependence on what others may think. When everyone else becomes the authority, we stay very small.

Sometimes we are hurt by trusting others too much and decide the only one we can trust is ourselves. We experience people as dangerous and unpredictable. Not trusting creates loneliness, lack of support, isolation, and defensiveness.

Lack of trust keeps us shut down, sad, unfulfilled, or stuck. Our Infant needs to hear trusting messages to rebuild her trust. That is one reason affirmations are so important in our personal growth. If these messages are not activated, critical judgmental messages come through and damage this beautiful, trusting part of us again and again. Because I was supposed to be a boy, my Infant self needs to hear the messages, "It is good to be a girl" and "I accept you just as you are," especially when I feel weak and untrusting.

Nancy is a thirty-six-year-old woman who did not trust others, especially men, and she felt stupid. She had been given up for adoption a month after she was born. Her trust was so violated by abuse throughout her life that if anyone did anything to threaten her trust, she left without giving him or her a chance and shut that person out completely. She felt very isolated, like she always has looked from the outside in, and felt that she didn't deserve love.

Nancy described herself as being surrounded by blackness because she had so much fear and guilt over what she has done to hurt others.

At a Woman Within Training, Nancy looked in a mirror and got reacquainted with the Infant inside her. As she looked deep into her eyes to catch a glimpse of her innocence and her goodness, tears streamed down her face. For the first time in her life, she fell in love with herself. Her infant self could now trust adult Nancy to take care of her needs and to trust others. Nancy visualized her infant surrounded by other women holding long-stemmed pink roses welcoming her Infant self into the world.

Affirmations for a Trusting Infant

- I trust myself to choose others to support and encourage me in my new experiences.

- I am a good mother to myself and feed my infant self positive messages.

- I listen to my body and trust what my body is telling me.

Questions and Exercises to Discover Your Infant Archetype
Think back to your own infancy and your first moments of birth. What were the first words written on your infant's blank page?

It serves you when you see each day as a blank page by asking, "How can my innocence serve me today?" "Who and what can fill up my blank page today?"

One way to examine your trust template is to think about your relationship history with men and women. Do you trust others? Do you trust yourself when you are with others? Is your trust different with women than with men? How do new situations affect you? Do you trust others to provide for your needs? Do you trust too much?

Do you trust too little?

Remember a time when you ignored your body and your needs. What happens when you do not listen to your body?

Take a moment to consider the infant stages of your ideas, relationships, or even personal changes—dieting, quitting smoking, or ending a relationship. In these Infant moments, how do you feel about others' judgments about what you are doing? Are you swayed or do you doubt yourself as you launch into "birth" moments of your life? Do you allow these moments to be aborted because you believe more in what others think than trust in your own thoughts?

When you access the Infant archetype, the first step is to scan your body for cues and clues that will tell you what you need. After finding sensations or discomfort in any part of your body, put a sound to what your body is telling you. Then express the sounds out loud. This exercise frees up your body and connects you with the purity of your Infant archetype.

When you feel you don't know enough to begin something new, check in with the innocent characteristic of this archetype and know that you can learn from others, from books, and from other resources to help you take the next step. Be receptive to everything around you: the junk mail, what you watch on television, or whom you meet during the day. Each of these may be the messenger and teacher for what you need to know next. By checking in with what you need and want, trust others to guide you.

Learn to trust others and yourself. Because of the makeup of your brain, your ability to relate and read body cues is your gift in knowing who to trust and what situations you can trust. When you feel helpless and dependent, your Infant is crying for you to surrender to the moment. Let your infant self tell you what she needs. Remember to listen to your body for messages about what your infant self wants, and take time to nurture and love her.

Thank the infant every day for all she provides to support you through the day and the passages of your life. Give her the gift of your attention and appreciation.

Kathy Entrup's Story

At a Woman Within Training I learned the importance of trust. When my mother was pregnant, she had an abortion. Little did my mother know that she was pregnant with twins, so I continued to grow in my mother's womb, all along knowing that I was unwanted and despised. Also, when I was a young girl I was sexually abused.

During a process when I got in touch with my loss, as well as my sexual abuse, I closed my eyes and the ground shifted under me. A facilitator had worked with me during some of my earlier processes and knew I was dealing with my mother's attempted abortion. She started talking to me and I felt as raw as a newborn. She encouraged me to open my eyes and I simply could not do it. What I know now to be dripping shame and permeating unworthiness kept my eyes closed. As I finally started to open my eyes, I saw the facilitator's eyes mirroring truth to me, and it was one of those moments that thoroughly changed my DNA and my core. "Corrective emotional experience" is what they call it in graduate school! It was the first and only time I had experienced a healthy connection, soul to soul, and for that I am eternally grateful.

I looked into the facilitator's eyes and I said, "I exist, I can be here, I belong here, I deserve to be here. I will be here with enough power for all of us." I anchored in my experience by imagining that I have a lighthouse within shining yellow light, set upon rocks, in choppy waters, and it's peaceful. Because of this experience I have a soft place in my heart for adolescent girls. The blindsiding of my mother's abortion, the loss of my twin, and my lack of trust all fell away and I was held by the facilitator's eyes.

At this moment I opened my eyes for the first time to the belief that it was okay for me to exist in this world. The facilitator's eyes saw me. I then existed. Existence was no longer a fight. I am here and no one can take me away. I am not my body. I am my spirit. I will not cease to exist.

I was welcomed by the facilitator's eyes! Her eyes didn't tell me who I was, they honored who I was. She looked into my eyes, was Present to me and still Welcomed me. The only condition was that I Exist. Her eyes expected that and welcomed me. I am no longer borrowing existence. I am Living Existence.

Chapter 4

Play with Your Magical Child

The discovery of the inner child is really
the discovery of a portal to the soul.
—Jeremiah Abrams

In every adult there lurks a child, an eternal child, something
that is always becoming, is never completed,
and calls for unceasing care, attention and education.
This is part of the human personality which wants
to develop and become whole.
—C. G. Jung

*As you continue to explore your sacred place, you hear laughter, music,
and the voices of children in the distance. Your step quickens almost to a
run as you follow the sounds to the place where your Inner Child dwells.
When you open the door, you see children of all ages playing together.
Each child is a part of you. You are amazed at the wonder and magic
of all these parts of yourself and delight in the happy and gleeful spirit
in your child's room.*

*W*e call on our Child archetype when we need to turn drudgery into play, impossible tasks into infinite possibilities, and our buried emotions into a healing flow of deep expressed feelings. Our Child can be a magical director of our lives when we invite her and listen to her.

Even when we do not call her forth, she is activated when we are threatened, and she shows up when we feel lighthearted and playful. Recalling memories from our childhoods help us reconnect with our Inner Child. Sometimes looking at photographs of ourselves helps us to connect with her. Even if we struggle with remembering our Inner Child, know that she is very much alive within us and is waiting to teach us how her characteristics can better our lives. As we recall images, either in our mind or with physical pictures, our Inner Child calls to us in our dreams and reveries.

In the 1990s the main focus in personal growth work was on the "wounded" child and all the trauma and abuse we endured. It strengthens us now to focus on the playful, loving, and magical child who got us through our pain and to use her positive characteristics to guide and transform us into wholeness.

Characteristics of the Child Archetype

Wants to Be Seen and Heard

Full of Wonder

Playful

Expressive

The Child Wants to Be Seen and Heard
As the infant grows into childhood and begins to talk and walk, she

continues to need love and attention in order to survive and grow. To feel loved, she wants to be seen and heard. When she is affirmed she learns how to nurture herself and step into who she is. Access to our Child archetype helps us flourish in our relationships, our businesses, even in the tumultuous times of our lives.

A child is required to learn thousands, if not millions of new tasks, such as controlling her bodily functions, feeding herself, socializing with others, perhaps giving over her space to a new sibling, communicating with words instead of crying, and discovering the hazards and limitations of her environment. Amidst all this learning, the child wants to be seen, heard, affirmed, and loved. This want stays with us throughout life; we find ways to modulate and change our behavior to get this.

As I watch my two granddaughters mature through their early childhood, I am amazed how each one becomes the center of her family. Every room of their houses reflects the presence of children, with toys, dress-up clothes, balls, and games. One of my sons hung a swing from the rafters of the living room so their daughter could swing at any time of the day. My other son remodeled their basement so his children could have a special place to play. Both sons used to sleep late; now they get up early to give attention to their daughters. Their focus is making sure their daughters are seen and heard by them.

Do we love our Inner Child this much? Loving and giving our Inner Child what she needs takes a lot of time and attention. If we did not get love and attention growing up as a child, we may resent giving what we did not receive. If our parents were alcoholic, too busy, ill, or for whatever reason not present to love and celebrate us, we tended to take charge and grow up really fast, leaving us feeling empty inside. If our parents abandoned us, we learned early to be self-sufficient. Perhaps we were super-achievers in school or sports or took over adult responsibilities at home, thereby missing out on the freedom and beauty of childhood. In this process we did not get to dwell in this room of our sacred place. That is why it is important to return and find our Inner Child and begin to recapture the lost days of play and wonder. If we do not return here, we might get stuck on filling our emptiness with giving others what we did not get in order to be seen and heard.

At the other end of the spectrum, if we got everything we wanted we likely did not learn how to take care of our needs and thus expect everyone to give us what we want. If our parents continually hovered over us and smothered us with attention, our skills of self-sufficiency might never have developed. We are pressured to meet our caregivers' high expectations so that we are acceptable and loved. We grow up trying to be perfect for everyone else and lose our sense of self. We perhaps spend many lonely nights and days trying to figure out where we fit in, and we feel like an adult extension of our parents. In this scenario, we never want to leave the child's room because it is too scary. As adult women, we continue to figure out what others expect of us and work very hard to meet everyone's ideals. We need to return to the child's room to let her know she can be her unique self and that she is okay just the way she is.

If we were not seen and heard as a child, we find ways to get noticed and be seen. As a child my parents were very busy and had little time to see me or listen to me. I felt invisible. One Sunday morning my parents were busy getting ready for church and I decided at three years of age to hide under a blanket in my brother's crib so my parents would have to work to see me. I could hear them calling my name. I was so happy—I could hear them calling my name! They searched for a long time and I could tell they were concerned—*They must love me*, I thought—they are worried. When they finally discovered me they were angry, and yes, I got attention, but not the attention I wanted. I repeated this behavior as an adult to get attention from my husband. When my husband was working for United Way as a loan executive, he was gone a lot and having a great time meeting new people, socializing, and having fun. I was feeling left out, unseen and lonely. So one night when he was out late, I decided to hide in a closet so when he came home he couldn't find me and then he would be worried and concerned and perhaps love me more. Of course, this behavior only made my husband angry and did nothing to satisfy my need to be seen and heard.

Now, since I have learned that my Child needs to be seen and heard, I listen to her and ask her what she needs. Now when I am feeling unseen and unloved, I simply ask my husband to look me in my eyes. When he stops what he is doing and stands and looks me in the eyes, I feel so affirmed that I usually begin to cry. This is what my Inner Child needed then—to be seen—and this is what she still needs in order to heal from years of being unheard and unseen.

Affirmations for a Child Wanting
to Be Seen and Heard

- I give my Inner Child all the attention she needs by listening to her and letting her know I love her.
- I ask for what I need from those who love me.

The Child Is Full of Wonder
To keep our minds alive and growing requires us to call on the childlike characteristic of wonder to explore new areas, learn new skills, and bring magic into our world. In childhood we experiment with numerous games, toys, and adventures to discover who we are. As a child we repeat skills again and again to master what we want to accomplish. When a child hears a story, she often says, "Read it

again, read it again!" As we become adults, we lose this childlike patience to learn a skill. If we want to learn a new language or skill, we may say to ourselves, "I am not talented here." How easy it is to forget how our brain grows: through practice and repetition. Children understand the learning curve. They are not afraid of failing and trying again and again. They are not ashamed to ask for help. Every time my granddaughter asks for help, I tell her to keep asking for help from a pure place of power. Learning how to learn is a powerful skill that sustains us our entire lives.

As children explore and learn, their creativity and magical thinking blossoms. A child creates through arts and crafts and often uses any available wall as a canvas. A banana can become a tent, or a doll, or something to smear on the table. Through the gift of creativity the mind develops, and it is also the time when boundaries are learned. It takes skill to learn how to be creative within the boundaries of society, authority figures, and our peers. Unfortunately, our society has put such stringent boundaries on our creative spirit that this characteristic is often repressed.

When we learn something new, it is our adult responsibility to use this skill to make our own and others' lives better. If we do not share what we have learned, we cheat ourselves and others. In my quest to write this book, I read hundreds of books, studied with many Jungian teachers, went to classes, listened to tapes, attended workshops, taught workshops; however, it took years before I was able to focus on writing a book. I was like a selfish child who had stored all this information in a secret closet. I needed to grow up, open my closet of my treasured knowledge, and begin to shape all the blocks, puzzles, and toys into something to be shared with others.

Perhaps we have become perpetual students or we are continually exploring many projects and ideas, loving the magic of learning, and we fail to bring what we have learned to the world. We get so stimulated by learning that we don't stop and rest and integrate. This can happen in personal growth work. Learning and changing can become addictive, and the "high" of growth propels us to want more and more and more until we realize the rest of our life has been put on hold. When we do not put what we learn into action, we stay stuck in our fantasy world. We need to plant our dreams in reality and start making them come true.

If our parents or caregivers were filled with fear, we may live a rigid, fear-based life and forget how magical our Inner Child is. When we are full of fear, it is difficult to take risks, try new things, ask questions, and fully express our creativity. Also, if we grew up in an alcoholic family or if one of our parents left through divorce or death, we may have lost the joy of exploring and learning. We become over-responsible and fail to expand our horizons.

In my family my parents always told me to clean my plate because there were starving children in the world who didn't have food. This made no sense to me, however, it did create fear inside of me. My parents had gone through the Great Depression and were just waiting for something bad to happen. Because of this underlying belief that there might not be enough, I did not feel free to be me and became fearful and hypervigilant. This lack of the magical Child archetypal energy keeps us stuck in jobs we hate or in unfulfilling relationships because we are afraid of being alone or impoverished.

As children, if we were not allowed to make a mess with paints, or dirt, or water, and we were forced to color within the lines, we shut the door to our Child's room and to our creativity, feelings, and imagination. To reclaim this part of ourselves, we can go back to this room and call to our magical Child and work with her to create new ways of being.

An example of how one woman found her Inner Child and worked with her magic to create a new reality for herself is Pam. When Pam was eight years old, her mother died, and she was not allowed to go to the funeral. Her family never talked about what happened, and Pam always blamed herself for her mother's death. From the moment of her mother's funeral, she made a decision never to allow herself to feel her pain and loss. Instead, she locked her grieving Inner Child securely away in a dark inner place—her dungeon. In doing this, she also locked up her magical, creative Child. As a result, Pam became an adult woman who did not use her imagination and did not express her feelings and longings, good or bad.

When she called on the magical archetypal Child at a Woman Within Training, Pam was able to rewrite the fairy tale of her sad childhood. She picked up her magic wand and found her Inner Child sitting on the dark stairs of her dungeon. She took little Pam out of the dungeon and into the sunshine where her mother was waiting for her. She imagined her mother holding little Pam and let all her grief tumble out of her body. Now little Pam can feel joy and can trust the adult Pam to never leave her again. A bright gold light entered Pam's soul, and she felt much lighter and optimistic about her future.

Be aware of how this magical energy may be hiding in your body. Many women have an undiscovered artist, author, musician, sculptor waiting to be discovered. Go on a treasure hunt and find her.

Affirmations for a Child Full of Wonder

- I am discovering and exploring new ideas every day.
- I use my imagination to bring magic into my own and other's lives.
- I am creative and have fun in all that I do.

The Child Knows How to Play

Watching and playing with my grandchildren wears me out, and I love every minute of it! They are constantly busy and doing some task all day long. The world of imagination is their school, and the result is lots of new synapses in their brains. One day, my three-year-old granddaughter played with a bag of ponytail elastics for an hour. She created a variety of games and ways of seeing this bunch of rubber bands that was way beyond my imagination. This ability to play, combined with her sense of wonderment, helps her brain to grow and develop.

Children put their whole bodies into what they are doing. My granddaughters don't just swim; they are fish or mermaids or dolphins. They don't just swing; they are astronauts, birds, or airplanes. They don't just dance; they are performers and stars and they love being in their bodies! Their bodies express joy through laughter, through raising their arms in the air, through the glimmer and light in their eyes. When they accomplish something, they raise their arms high above their heads and say, "Ta da!"

How many of us have lost the joy of play and fantasy that awakens all kinds of possibilities? When we reclaim this characteristic, we can access our spontaneity to propel us forward into new areas of our life.

Children are not only playing, they are having fun at their work of play. As adults, we seek the balance between work and play. At times we would rather play than work. When this happens, we may become irresponsible and shun tasks that need to be done—like taxes. Consider a woman who is fun to be with, joyful, and enjoys her work. She is very creative; however, she hates to write reports and follow through with paperwork. Her Child rules her life and gets very stubborn when any paperwork is required. She doesn't file her taxes for years and eventually has to file bankruptcy. Her Child—not the balanced adult woman—is ruling her life.

If we were not allowed to play as children, we may not know how to play as adults. Growing up in a Baptist minister's home restricted my ability to play and have fun. Because my dad's study was in our house, I could play as long as I was very quiet. Sitting still in school five days a week and then sitting still in church twice on Sunday and every Wednesday night restricted the time I had to play, to explore, be spontaneous, and creative. I spent a lot of time alone and never learned how to play.

When we fail to build play, fun, and spontaneity into our lives and become too serious, we end up being bored and depressed. Everything becomes a chore, and we feel like we are moving through sludge. When worry and strain consumes us, it is time to call on our archetypal playful Child to teach us how to play and let ourselves go. Learning to let our Child archetype teach us how to play may at first seem like work. However, play can lighten our load and free up our spirit. Start slowly. Start small, and let the Child part of you have a day of play.

Affirmations for a Playful Child

- I expand my imagination through play.
- I am spontaneous and joyful
- I balance my work with time to play.

The Child Is Expressive

A child develops her intellect through hours of exploring and learning about science, history, math, and many other areas. She also is learning how to express her feelings through words as she develops her emotional self. As an infant, she expressed her feelings through sounds and facial expressions. Now by developing her emotional intelligence, she begins to add words to her nonverbal expression. She learns how to use her voice in a new way to get what she wants.

She learns her feeling vocabulary from the adults around her, television, and her peers. All of these are role models in teaching her how to express emotions, and she needs to learn how to express herself in a clean, healthy way. When we express emotions cleanly, we state what we feel without blaming someone else. A child learns to name her feelings as simple as being sad, mad, glad, or scared, and then she needs to hear her parents and other adults reflect these feelings back to her.

The way to teach a child a feeling vocabulary is through the skill of listening and repeating back what the child said. Take, for example, my granddaughter, who is really upset that she is not getting something she wants. She starts screaming, "I hate you!" Instead of her parents telling her, "Don't talk to us like that," they say, "You really are mad and disappointed that you can't have what you want." This way of communicating diffuses the intense emotion and teaches her how to name and express what she is feeling.

In the same way, we need to listen to our Inner Child. Most of us were never taught how to identify our feelings; we denied them because we did not know how to express them in a direct clear manner. When our emotions are triggered, it is common for us to respond as a child. For example, when my emotions are triggered, I tend to respond by going silent. When I find myself responding in this way, I remember to parent my Inner Child by listening to her instead of shutting her up or letting her take over. The healthy, balanced Child in me has to be taught how to put into words what she is feeling. If you were never listened to by the adults in your life, this will take practice. Sometimes this may require a therapist to listen to your Inner Child so you can learn to express your feelings and wants cleanly and clearly. The simple skill of listening is the most difficult and the most healing communication skill. The healthy child can express feelings and then move back into spontaneous play and learning.

If we were threatened, traumatized, or humiliated for expressing our feelings when we were a child, we may grow up as quiet and reserved. Instead of expressing our feelings outward, we submerge and stuff them, becoming depressed because it takes so much energy to keep all of our feelings buried.

When we are with someone whom we feel has more authority than us, we may be unable to express ourselves. I consider myself a rather evolved woman; however, I was unable to express myself at a recent doctor's visit. The doctor, being the authority in relationship to my health, was showing signs of incompetence, like not having my proper records, asking me confusing questions, and not ordering the lab work I needed. She responded to my inquiry about a fax I sent two weeks ago with, "Oh, I have a two-foot high pile of correspondence on my desk." I was livid. I thought the doctor was discounting me and I felt sad and angry. I felt unsafe and I felt little. Instead of being an adult woman and requesting her to find my records and order my lab work, my naïve child took over and acted very stupid and compliant. I am a nurse, and I am not naïve or stupid. But the power of the Child archetype ruled in the face of the authority of the doctor.

Child archetypal energy overtook me before I knew what was happening. In retrospect, when I recognized what was happening, I could have closed my eyes, taken some deep breaths, and called in the energy of my expressive Child to state what I needed in a firm confident manner. When we are in a place where we feel very small and young, we need to take a moment to give expression to our Child's feelings by using "clean" words to express what is going on inside us.

Affirmations for an Expressive Child

- I express my feelings cleanly.
- I ask for others to hear me when I am upset or angry.
- I listen to my Inner Child.
- I give my Inner Child the time and space she needs.

Questions and Exercises to Discover Your Child Archetype
Your Need to Be Seen and Heard
Remember you always need to be seen and heard. Ask for what you want. You might even consider asking for a *surprise* birthday party and get a lot of attention!

Think of a scene in your adult life when you did not feel seen or heard. Be aware of the feelings that come up in your body as you recall this incident. What did you do? Were you trying to take care of everyone else while feeling empty and alone inside? Did you suppress the pain and act tough? How did you get the love and attention you were craving? How could you script this scene differently using what you know now?

Your Sense of Wonder
Know that the best antidote for growing old is to keep alive the Child's need to learn and explore. You are never too old to learn new things and adventure into unexplored territory. Try something new once a month. Create an exciting fun-filled life for yourself.

Call upon the imagination of your Child to create solutions to very difficult problems. Is there any area in your life that could use the characteristic of exploring and learning? If you don't get something the first time, do you give up? How can you call on the Child archetype to keep going with a task of learning something new?

Your Ability to Play

When you are feeling lonely and isolated, call in the Child who knows how to play, have fun, and create magic in your life. Invoke her energy to dance, to laugh, to be spontaneous, to play games, or have a tea party with friends.

When was the last time you let play help you discover another way of doing something? As an adult woman, have you lost this joy in your work life and play life? Can you imagine how free you could feel if you let spontaneous play seep out of your body every day? Do you love what you do? Does your work seem like play?

How can your creative spirit be set free? Spend a day with a child and let her lead you in play. Watch how she creates magic in every moment from how she makes bubbles in her milk to how she becomes a frog in the tub. Take notes and then go out and let this archetype take over to create more magic in your life.

Your Ability to Be Expressive

The Child in you wants to express her feelings. Although this isn't always appropriate in an adult setting, acknowledge the truth of what you are feeling through journaling, therapy, or simply stopping long enough to ask the question, "What is the pure essence of what I am feeling right now?"

Think back to a time when you were hurting as a child. What did you say and do at this time? Were you heard? If not, take a moment to visualize your Child and let her express her feelings about this situation. As she expresses them, repeat back to her what you hear, using feeling vocabulary.

Alison Davis' Story

I now know that the Child archetype is constantly at work in my life and I am in touch with this archetype as a powerful pattern. I am aware of her many aspects, such as my wounded Child, my abandoned Child, my innocent Child, and my Divine Child. All these energies are alive inside me and manifest themselves depending on the kind of situations in which I find myself.

I have found that exploring the Child archetype within me has awakened a new relationship with life, which feels like a fresh beginning. It has brought me more into contact with my creativity. I know that this is the core of my innocent Child—the sensation that anything and everything is possible. My mother was always very busy and worried a lot about us making a mess in the house, so I wasn't encouraged to be creative. The fact that I was never encouraged in this—even criticized for dressing up and told that I wasn't creative—meant that I had difficulty being creative as an adult or giving myself permission to try. It was only in the past ten years that I discovered that I was very creative, and, much to my surprise, I even won a national award for interior design!

My Inner Magical Child has helped me to catch up with the exploring and learning I didn't do as a child. I love going to courses and learning new things.

Children have a natural wish to live in their bodies and don't have the inhibitions about this that we sometimes develop later on. I was never encouraged to live in my body. I loved to skip and dance to music. Our house had a long corridor with a mirror at one end. I loved walking down this corridor toward the mirror pretending I was a film star. If my mother caught me looking in the mirror, she told me it was bad to be vain. My father was self-conscious about his body, so watching them and hearing their recommendations taught me to disconnect with my body and become self-conscious too. It's taken work as an adult to overcome those inhibitions. These days I very often give myself permission to skip for joy!

As a child I loved to play. I wanted to be a fashion model, but my mom thought playing at this was vain. So when I got to stay with my granny in the summer, I persuaded her to lend me all her beautiful clothes, high-heeled shoes, and fur hats, and I created a fashion parade with my sisters! I thought I looked fabulous! It was during moments such as these that I was really in touch with my magical Child. Today I am able to connect back to how it felt during these moments, and this can give me confidence to "dare to be fully myself" in my life.

Nowadays as an adult, the Child in me still enjoys my toys! I have crystals, card decks, aromatherapy bottles, makeup … that provide me with endless happy hours of entertainment when I allow myself to indulge!

As I look back on these childhood passions, I find they tell me a lot about who I am. They are the golden threads or interrupted dreams of my life that have shed a lot of light on what is my ideal work.

I can still find it difficult to play or forget to play and have fun as an adult. This is something we all need to do whatever age we are. It releases stress and helps us become more creative and feel more alive. What I've done in recent years is to seek out friends who know how to do this and I've learned by spending time hanging out with them!

As I've learned to heal and balance my inner child I am able to see the potential for sacred beauty in all things as I hold the belief that anything is possible. I know that at these times I can be enchanting to others too. I can be spontaneous when I allow myself to be.

Chapter 5

Move through Transitions with Your Adolescent

It is the twilight zone between past and future that is the precarious
world of transformation within the chrysalis.
Part of us is looking back, yearning for the magic we have lost;
part is glad to say good-bye to our chaotic past;
part looks ahead with whatever courage we can muster;
part is excited by the changing potential;
part sits stone-still not daring to look either way.
—Marion Woodman

*As you walk through your sacred place you come to a room where the
ground seems to be shifting under your feet. Each step you take brings a
change to your equilibrium and you are not sure where to step next. A
part of you wants to go back to the safety of the Child's room, and yet
part of you is intrigued and excited about all the risks and challenges of
this shifting, changing adventure. Welcome to the Adolescent archetypal
energy that emerges every time you go through a transition from one
phase of your life to another.*

*A*dolescence is a time of transition, a threshold, an opportunity to pass from an old way of being to a totally new experience. This archetype is activated when we enter a space between two ways of being, called a "liminal space." A liminal space is like a doorway or a threshold, and as soon as we pass through or over we have left the old and entered a new way of being. While standing in the doorway we feel off balance and unsure of what step to take next. Our heads feel confused because we have entered unknown territory. These threshold experiences happen when we leave a job or career and start a new one. They happen when we move from being single into partnering or when we go from partnering to being single. Becoming a mother for the first time is a huge transition. This happens when we experience a midlife crisis. We all face many transitions in our lives, and the Adolescent archetype is there to help us through them. If we fail to acknowledge and work with the Adolescent archetype, our passage may be disrupted and difficult.

Characteristics of the Adolescent Archetype

Transitions from Old to New

Navigates Change

Separates from Authority

Explores Identity and Relationships

The Adolescent Transitions from the Old to the New
When we are transitioning to something new and different, we need to call on the Adolescent archetype to be with us. These times require us to become like a caterpillar crawling on the ground. We feel unsure, perhaps scared and low (or depressed). As we walk along, we have an urge to get through this stage fast so we can soar

and fly, forgetting that it is important for us to go through this change consciously. This means we need to give up dreaming about flying and find a safe place to weave a cocoon around ourselves and stay put for a while. We need time alone. We need to leave behind what others are telling us about this passage. It is time to figure out who we are becoming and stay in our cocoons away from the criticism, judgments, and advice of others. To our friends and family, it looks like we are disconnecting, and we are! To some, we may look depressed, like a social recluse—somebody needing help. To us, it is a time to transform into something new.

A transitional time for me was when my sons were no longer little boys. They had become men; however, I needed to transition from being mother to my sons to learning a how to relate to them as grown men. My old way wanted them to stay little boys so that I could be fulfilled as their mother. However, they are no longer little boys—they are men. Yes, I am their mother; however, barraging them with calls, e-mails, and texts does not serve them. I need to find my place on the shifting ground. When I go into my cocoon I learn who I am apart from being a mother of little boys and realize that when I emerge as a mother of grown men, I will be different. I can fly when I stop giving them unsolicited advice, nagging them to stay in contact with me, and begin relating to them as adult to adult. When we are in our cocoons, we don't know what the new will look like, and yet we know that the old must die in order to transform.

This transformation is like a rite of passage that requires separation, suffering, conflict, and a return. By going through the suffering, we develop courage, strength, and compassion. The caterpillar has to encase herself into a chrysalis and literally dissolve the "worm" part of her to emerge a beautiful butterfly. Perhaps that is why young teenage girls struggle with their body image when they develop breasts, acne appears, hair gets oily, and they often feel ugly and want to hide from others. The result is pain, ambivalence, and confusion. These are all normal changes during transitions. It is important not to ignore these changes and to acknowledge why they are necessary. This is not only a period of transition; it is a period of change. Just like lobsters and snakes shed their protective covering so they can grow up—grow bigger—so does transition require the vulnerability of losing what is comfortable and known, yet very tight and restricting, so that a new shell or skin can be created. As this process takes place, there are many risks inherent because of our vulnerability. Some of these risks are depression, acting out our fears, and even suicide. This is why so many adolescent songs and poems are obsessed with death and the color black. These same risks are inherent in all of our transitions.

The time in the chrysalis is a slow, painful death of who we once were. For the adolescent it is the death of being a child. It may be the death of being a single woman or the death of being a working woman or the death of being a student. The expectation of the Adolescent archetype is extraversion; however, the struggle to become requires periods of introversion to obtain balance. Thus, retreating to our sacred place, closing our door, and being in our cocoon alone is part of the process. The forces of the outside world may tend to push and pull us to come out of our cocoons before it is time. However, when the Adolescent archetype enters, we must enter our chrysalis so we can transform.

Although the chrysalis appears motionless, there is a lot of activity going on inside. The anatomy of the caterpillar is being reorganized into an adult butterfly. During this time it is easy prey because it has few defenses and is unable to fly. This is a complicated stage of change. Even as the caterpillar secretes hormones to form the chrysalis, so does an adolescent. In other words, we must want to grow up and change so much that we are willing to give up being a child in order to become an adult. The challenge is to stay in the chrysalis long enough for nature to take its course so we can emerge as beautiful butterflies.

What happens if we let others mess with our protective covering to see how we are progressing or help us come out of our cocoon before it is time? This destroys the process of transformation and results in death of the new. The struggle to transform from a caterpillar to a butterfly requires change and time, and it isn't pretty. When the butterfly emerges, its wings are soft and weak.

One way of assisting us in these transitions is to go on a vision quest. This is a Native American ritual in which the participants go into nature alone and fast for three days (or longer) to get a vision of who they are to become. This process requires a separation from the old and an ordeal, that is, going through the fear of the dark, fear of the elements and other realities of nature, and then returning to a new life and being welcomed by a community. The major task of this process is to overcome and walk through the fear of moving from one state of being to another. This takes a lot of elasticity of movement, meaning going forward, backward, and sideways.

If we get stuck in this archetype, we continually ask the question, "What am I going to be when I grow up?" Instead of cocooning, we refuse to go into the chrysalis, and instead of growing up, we remain stuck in the old. In Jungian psychology the archetype of a woman who doesn't want to grow up or grow old is called *puella eterna,* and she is fixated at the girlish level of development. When this happens we deny the negative parts of life and focus only on the positive. We are unable to adapt and change. One way this shows up is that we assume a passive role in our intimate relationships by always choosing partners to parent us. Psychologically we remain an immature Adolescent, stuck in the Child archetype.

This pattern can be seen in many stages of a woman's development. For instance, some older women attempt to dress like adolescents because they do not want to accept that they are getting older, thinking perhaps that if they dress like they feel inside, they will be perceived as younger. The truth is, when a woman stays stuck in her development, she is like a caterpillar in the chrysalis that cannot complete her transformation into a butterfly. She is imprisoned by the process instead of letting herself surrender to the pain of transformation in a conscious way. Her chrysalis becomes her prison, and even though she hates its boundaries and limits, she is smothered by them. Emotionally, she remains an Adolescent who is continually seeking to find who she is and she avoids responsibility. Søren Kierkegaard calls this dilemma "The Despair of Weakness: the despair of not willing to be oneself." The woman knows only how to be what others want her to be. Therefore, she focuses only on her weakness and her inability to get out of the chrysalis and becomes a victim of her childhood.

To emerge from this stuck place, a woman needs to accept that she has the strength to do so from a higher part of herself and accept the suffering needed to emerge from this prison. The *puella* tends either to run away from difficult situations or to rebel against them. When a woman realizes that she is truly powerful, has a voice, and begins to value herself, the *puella* no longer has a hold on her. She can then emerge from the chrysalis and become the butterfly. Emergence from the chrysalis requires us to break down old attitudes and beliefs so we can emerge into a new way of being.

Michael Gurian in his study of adolescent girls shares in his book, *The Wonder of Girls,* that if the adolescent girl is guided to navigate this passage with safety, innocence, and attachments to her parents, she develops into a stronger, more competent twenty-five-to thirty-year-old than if she were forced to mature early.

When the transformation is not allowed to progress naturally, we tend to shut down our emotions and disconnect from our bodies. It becomes too difficult to stay the course of transformation, and we look for ways to numb our pain and ignore our changes. We fail to listen to what our body needs and forget to love our body *just as it is* through all its changes. If we ignore our changes, we remain fragile and insecure and we do not become unique and independent.

Although the Adolescent archetype requires us to become self-centered, staying in the process of discovery can overtake and consume us. If we refuse to move through transitions and think we know who we are, we may experience a false self covering up our true self. One way this shows up is as postpartum depression. Although a woman has nine months to experience all the physical changes in her body, read books, and prepare for her baby, there is no preparation that truly prepares her to step into the mother role at the moment of the baby's birth. Suddenly, she is consumed by this little one and has little to no time for herself, her partner, or her career. Depression takes over because the mother thought she was prepared and finds herself off balance in her new role.

Consider Janice, who just gave birth to her child by C-section. Three days after coming home from the hospital, she hosted an open house for neighbors, friends, and family. All day long she smiled and kept a happy (false) face and pretended to be cheerful. Inside, she was exhausted, depressed, and worn out, yet no one knew. Her archetypal "good girl" took over, and Janice was being who she thought her guests expected her to be. Instead of taking time to go into her chrysalis so she could integrate all her new feelings of becoming a mother, which were feelings of depression, overwhelm, and exhaustion, she pretended to be a "joyful butterfly," all the time destroying her vulnerable cocoon. Once the guests left, she broke down and cried for hours.

The Adolescent archetype experiments with new ways of being. This time of experimentation may become more than just trying drugs or exploring sexuality. Experimenting with drugs and alcohol is a search for the new "spirit," which may turn dangerous because it takes the Adolescent archetypal energy away from the self instead of toward the new self. Exploring sexuality may result in getting pregnant or getting taken advantage of. When the experimenting becomes an addiction, the Adolescent archetype is in danger of death and disease.

When we move toward something new, such as a new relationship, we may want to experiment with new ways of being and acting. This can activate the Adolescent archetype that knows no boundaries and loves the thrill of the moment. The consequences cannot be seen immediately, and we may find ourselves in situations that we may later regret.

Kathleen, a participant at a Woman Within Training, was feeling rejected by her husband and alone. Before she came to the Training, she had felt strange sexual stirrings of her Adolescent archetype and was having an affair. She had bought new sexy underwear, did marginally dangerous things to have a rendezvous with her new lover, and was totally consumed by her desires and impulses. She truly wanted a new relationship with her husband, yet instead of exploring how to move into that, she moved instead into a situation in which she was tested, and, in the long run, hurt and ashamed of what she had done. At the Training she was able to accept herself, forgive herself, and release the old pattern of looking for the exciting sexual charge. She committed to find a way to communicate to her husband her desire to be an adult in their relationship and ask for what she wants around her sexual needs.

Affirmations for an Adolescent Transitioning
from the Old to the New

- I make time to be alone in my cocoon when I go through transitions.

- I surrender my old way of being so I can become something new.

- I am vulnerable and I protect myself.

- I am aware of the risks and navigate my passage with grace and support.

- I adapt to the changes in my life by using rituals to mark my passages.

The Adolescent Navigates Changes

When we invite in the Adolescent archetype we need to rethink all we have ever thought to be true in the past. This process requires energy, the need to ask questions, to argue and to verbalize what we are thinking, as well as spending many hours alone to sort out who we are and what we need to do next. Because of the enormity of this task, we may have feelings of chaos, confusion, isolation, and loneliness.

Added to rethinking everything she has ever thought, the adolescent is also going through enormous biological changes: her breasts grow, pubic hair sprouts, and she starts menstruating, her skin changes, and the cells in her brain double. The mirror may reflect the image of a child or it may reflect the image of an adult woman. During puberty everything is changing, and she is still a little girl becoming an adult, making her very vulnerable. Coupled with the physical changes are emotional changes. She becomes emotionally fragile. This phenomenon can be seen when a woman gets pregnant and when she goes through menopause. The questions of "Who am I? Where am I headed?" are important to ask and meditate on when we face transitions.

All transitions require change. How we experienced change in our adolescence will affect how we experience changes in our life today. What we cared about in early adolescence will be carried with us throughout our adult life. The only constant in life is change, so expecting and accepting change is a great gift of the Adolescent archetype that we can give ourselves to propel us forward through life.

There is a difference between expecting change and accepting change. When we go through a transition, it is valuable to have an idea of what we will be facing. Getting advice from those who have "been there and done that" is very valuable in knowing what to expect. However, accepting that these things will happen is very different. As a new mother, I never took the time or the energy to find women who were already mothers and talk to them about what to expect. All of my friends were either pregnant or still single. Isn't it interesting that we call this time of pregnancy "expecting," yet many of us don't know what to expect?

Once the changes happen, the challenge is to accept them. The Adolescent archetype gives us many opportunities to accept the changes that are happening to us and around us. When the change is accepted, we make strides toward a new way of being that can serve us. Accepting the change requires us to surrender to the unknown and let ourselves evolve moment by moment, choice by choice, and action by action.

If we resist change, we remain confused and we either move backward or stay stuck. Staying stuck takes a lot of energy, because our psyche wants and needs us to move forward. Nothing is static. Marion Woodman in her book *Conscious Femininity* states that when a woman resists change, she is like a confused butterfly that still thinks like a caterpillar and wants to go back into the nonexistent chrysalis instead of letting her beautiful wings unfold.

As a young adolescent, I resisted the changes in my body and hated my growing breasts. I wanted to cut them off. I didn't want to wear a bra, and I wanted to hide all signs of my blossoming femininity. It was not safe to talk to anyone about this secret desire or to let anyone know how much I hated my body. Today, as an adult, I continue to struggle with changes in my body, particularly those related to aging. I want to ignore the reality that my body is wrinkled and my breasts are sagging. Life is full of changes, and the stubborn, rebellious Adolescent in me does not want anything to change. As a way to grow up this part of me, I accept my changes as a normal part of my age and take every measure I can to look my best as an older woman. I also ask for advice and mentoring so I don't have to keep a secret or stay in denial. Remaining stuck in stifling relationships, clinging to the old, and hanging on to the "toys" of the past causes us to cling to the familiar instead of taking on the agony of change.

Instead of resisting change, we may let change consume us. Too much change too fast confuses us. We become flooded with emotions that we do not know how to handle, particularly if we have not learned coping mechanisms to do so. When we don't know how to cope, we experiment and make poor decisions too quickly. During change, emotions can run very high. When the Adolescent archetype takes over and we are flooded with emotions, we may scream, curse, cry, and act out. Learning how to express these feelings appropriately is the task of this archetype. Repressing them without expression can be just as dangerous as expressing them inappropriately. The option is containment, which means to acknowledge our feelings, name them, breathe through them, and express them in a healthy way to a therapist or trusted friend.

Writing them in a journal is an excellent way to contain and move through these feelings during change.

Affirmations for an Adolescent Navigating Change

- I accept the changes transformation brings and move through them.
- As I transition, I ask for support from those who know and understand.
- I am patient with my changing self.

The Adolescent Separates from Authority
The Adolescent archetype helps us take steps toward knowing our Inner Queen by discovering what we value and believe, so that we can find our own *inner* authority apart from all the other authorities in our life. The voices of our outer authorities, whether they are parents, our partners, teachers, or other peers, can be so loud that they drown out the evolving inner authority of the Adolescent archetype. Often, in order to find this voice, we must denounce all that *was* in order to find what *is* truly ours. Transitions require us to be grounded in our inner authority as we leave our known place and go into an unknown place.

My dad was a Southern Baptist minister, so I was challenged to find my own religious beliefs. After high school I attended a Baptist college where I was surrounded by a community who thought like my parents, and I was required to attend chapel twice a week. After my junior year, I transferred to a private university, where I was surrounded by a diverse community with religious beliefs that ranged from atheism to Catholicism to Hinduism. I was appalled when I found out my roommate was a Catholic, because I had been taught that Catholics were not Christians and were going to hell. As I examined these beliefs, I realized I could not accept the beliefs of my childhood and had to start all over. I had to throw out all my old religious beliefs and find a spiritual belief system that works for me.

As girls and women, culture has taught us to be silent and not to express our thoughts or even to know what we think and know as uniquely us. The Adolescent archetype allows us to test the waters of what feels right and rebel against what feels untrue in our hearts.

In their book *Female Authority,* Polly Young-Eisendrath and Florence Wiedemann define *female authority* as "the ability of a woman to validate her own convictions of truth, beauty and goodness in regard to her self-concept and self-interest." This is accomplished through recognizing and learning how to trust what is true for us, understanding the power of emotional expressiveness, and recognizing the power of our knowing.

If we fail to test our beliefs and take from our past what feels right as we move forward into the future, we will lose our uniqueness and true selves. Thus the Adolescent archetype allows us to distinguish ourselves from our parents, our partners, our children, our bosses, and our peers and accept our own unique qualities.

There is a danger in not pursing our separation, which Kierkegaard describes as three types of despair: unconscious despair, despair that is conscious and comes across as weakness, and despair that is conscious and manifests as defiance. When the despair comes across as weakness, we feel incompetent and are unable to move out of the force field of whomever we have put in an authority position. This happens with young adults who continue to live at home and find they are unable to assume responsibility for what they think and feel apart from their parents.

This attribute of the Adolescent archetype can also hold a woman in a dangerous, abusive relationship, whether personal or at work. Walking away from an abusive situation means we have to summon up the courage of our Inner Warrior to claim our inner authority because it takes commitment and courage to reclaim what is true for us.

In Kierkegaard's forms of despair, one that is also very evident in the adolescent archetype is that of rebelling, or as Kierkegaard describes, defiance. This shows up as stating so loudly what we believe that we lose all respect and sense of others around us. Some women rebel by rejecting the feminine part of them and become identified with their masculine energy.

If our fathers neglected us or weren't emotionally present for us, we may develop a skewed sense of strength and responsibility. We appear as strong; however, underneath our strong defiance lay insecurity and fragility. When this happens we work very hard to keep others from seeing how insecure we really feel. One way we act this out is to rebel against all authority and not even stop to consider how this rebellion may not serve us in the long run.

Susan was sexually abused by her father from the age of eight through her early adolescence. In order to survive this painful experience, she developed an attitude that nothing was going to get to her and no one knew better than her. Thus, all her relationships tended to fail, and throughout adulthood she was never able to develop satisfying intimate relationships. If anyone tried to challenge Susan's beliefs, she became very defensive and would stomp out of the room in rage. At a Woman Within Training, Susan went into the painful chrysalis and reclaimed her innocent Child and felt the feelings of betrayal and loss. As she was guided through her cocoon, she shed her armor of having to always protect herself from men hurting her. By recognizing how she was possessed by her fear and anger around men, she began to soften and listen to the opinions and ideas of others around her.

Affirmations for an Adolescent
Separating from Authority

- I value what I believe and who I am.
- I respect those in authority and I do not reject what I believe.
- I hear and respond to my inner authority.

The Adolescent Explores Relationships

As we separate from authority figures, find our own unique voice and way of being, we find ourselves faced with another challenge of navigating our relationships with our parents, our friends, and our intimate companions. Because the Adolescent archetype wants to be like others and at the same time wants to be different, she struggles to find a balance by experimenting, getting caught up in what others want, and feeling the pain of having to separate again. When we find ourselves in new territory, the temptation of listening to what others want us to be can be overwhelming and captivating. There is positive peer pressure, when others can give you reasons to think like they think and model for you who you can become, thus giving you a choice.

When we change careers, end one relationship and go into a new relationship, or move from one city to another, this archetype gets activated and we look for ways to fit in and belong. In her book *Queen Bees and Wannabees,* Rosalind Wiseman talks about the importance of friendships to survive transitions. In new relationships, it is normal to compare ourselves to others. Achieving stable, healthy relationships is one of the most important goals of the Adolescent archetype.

If we are too afraid or ill equipped to explore relationships, we become loners and isolate ourselves. When we make the transition into the new, we need a community of people so we can explore and learn more about ourselves. By letting others be a mirror for our behavior, we are able to capture our true essence. Without this, we become lost and alone and perhaps depressed about all the newness we are experiencing.

Take Beth, for example, who was recently diagnosed with breast cancer. She was consumed with fear and didn't want anyone to know she had breast cancer because she believed it would stimulate their fear and cause her to fear even more. She decided she would go through this time of surgery, chemo, radiation, and hormones alone. She did not have a container of friends and family to support her and she sank into a deep depression, which only made her recovery slower and more difficult. When she realized that perhaps she needed support of others besides the medical providers, she began to reach out and ask for support and understanding. Although she wasn't establishing new relationships, she was using her relationships in a new way. Beth had always been the one to support others, and now the tables were turned and she was the one needing support.

At the other extreme of refusing to enter into new relationships is entering into abusing relationships. We let our Adolescent archetype take over when we act out sexually to get attention. Adolescents are flooded with sexual energy; they are learning how their bodies respond, yet they do not know how to monitor or manage all these feelings. As adults we may jump from one relationship to another, trying to get attention by manipulating and cajoling others. We may become impulsive and lead what we think is a wild, exciting life. When we are abusing relationships in this way, it is very difficult for us to commit to anyone for very long. Instead of being cautious, we may take risks that can be dangerous and lead to destructive behavior.

Affirmations for an Adolescent Exploring Relationships

- I am aware and conscious of how I navigate the relationships with my peers.
- I go into relationships to learn about myself.
- I value my relationships and ask for support and guidance when needed.

Questions and Exercises to Discover Your Adolescent Archetype
Take a moment to remember what it was like being an adolescent and all the differences you experienced as a child moving into adulthood. Do you remember what your room looked like? When did your body start changing and what was that like? Recall your emotions and moods. Were you a rebellious or compliant adolescent, or were you both? What were your struggles and your achievements? Spend some time with this part of you, which took at least eight years to transition. She has a lot to teach you about the Adolescent archetypal energy and what gifts and barriers she may continue to bring you as an adult woman.

How were you told that changes were going to happen to your body? Was this a pleasant or scary experience? How would you have liked this stage of your life to have been different? Take a moment to journal what it was like growing breasts, starting your period, and going through these early years of adolescence.

Take moments to think back to your adolescence and how you reacted to the changes that were going on. Was there a mentor there to guide you and help you see the beauty of what was happening in your life? If not, this is an area you need to explore when you go through transitions, big and small.

Create an initiation ritual for your adolescent self to celebrate the beginning of your menses. Gather together a community of women that you trust to honor and celebrate you.

Create an initiation ritual to mark your transitions, such as graduation from school, becoming a mother, starting a new job, moving to a new home or city.

Are there areas in your life that are changing and you are not moving with the change? How can you support yourself (and your Inner Adolescent) through this period?

Write a letter of advice to yourself and ask your mentors to write one to you when you are experiencing or anticipating a transition.

Take time during your days of menstruation to listen to yourself and to reflect on who you are. If you are no longer menstruating, calendar an "introvert" day or time to be alone.

Go to some place in nature and walk alone for one day without food. Journal and observe nature and animals.

Take a moment to recall a time when you perhaps lost yourself to another person's opinion, belief, or way of thinking. What was it like to not trust what you truly believed and to agree with something that was contrary to your very soul? What messages were you telling yourself about you? Check in with your body as to how that felt.

Amy Pershing's Story

In my family, being good was far more important than being authentic. Conflict was dangerous; raised voices and dissent were cause for shame. When I hit adolescence and began to explore the big questions about who I was and who I might become, my little girl archetype was simply terrified. Here was this newfound teenager, a seemingly unstoppable questioner and rule breaker, someone who made impulsive choices and hung out with the "bad" kids. Who was this? My little girl was uncertain how she could continue to be loved with this new presence threatening her worth and value in the eyes of my parents.

My adolescent was indeed something to fear for that little girl. Anything that smacked of being "good," of following the rules, had to be challenged, be the challenge true to my heart or not. My adolescent could spot hypocrisy and inauthenticity a hundred miles away, and she would hone in with lightning speed to attack it. I wore nothing but black, smoked, drank, tried drugs, chased after the bad boys. All the while that little girl inside was terrified and ashamed, certain she would be shunned and excluded. I felt trapped between a teenager trying to separate from her family and a child uncertain that she could be loved by anyone if not good and perfect. I was too rebellious for my parents and not rebellious enough for my friends. My little girl was not getting it right with anyone. And my teenager was angry with this sniveling, anxious little child inside.

For me, this internal war was waged through my relationship with food. My eating disorder began in earnest when my adolescent came onto the scene. I had been dieting since a very early age (at about ten years old I went on my first restriction program, Scarsdale); being good with regard to food meant sticking to a program and losing weight. When my teenager showed up, how better for her to defy the powers that be than to binge? Binge eating became my way of breaking every rule, of eating anything my taste desired in the moment, with no care for consequence (or indeed unconsciously creating the worst rebellion of all, that of weight gain). It was the epitome of the Adolescent energy.

Following a binge the little girl felt incredible shame and guilt. She would now gain weight; she was without willpower, without the goodness inherent (so she was told) in being thin. So I would recommit all my energy to a new day, to a new diet. So the yo-yo went, for the next twenty years.

It was not until I understood how to call on my adult archetypes that I could truly address the needs of the Adolescent or the Child and stop enacting this battle with my body. Now in my mid-forties, I have given up the pursuit of making my body something it is not. I listen to my body's needs as I listen to those of my Adolescent and my Child. I am not a "good" girl, nor do I rebel for the sake of rebellion. I have a little girl and a teenager, and they are vocal about their ideas, their dreams, and their needs. I listen, from my adult self, as best I can. And I love them, as best I can.

I now run an eating disorder clinic and am very active in eating disorder treatment and advocacy efforts, especially for binge eating disorder. I know that without the presence of my Adolescent, I could not do this work. She helps me keep my voice, be true to what I know my clients need, and gives me a nudge to advocate for others who desperately need treatment to reclaim their own voices. I am grateful too for my ability to finally keep her safe. It has been a long road for me to be able to fully understand my Adolescent archetype and how she needs to be heard and seen. I now know all she did to protect me, to save my voice, when I was unable to do so directly. Without her coming out, albeit sometimes sideways, all in black, and with a practiced snarl, I would never have survived. I am grateful.

Chapter 6

Connect with Your Lover

To love yourself is the beginning of a lifelong romance.
—Oscar Wilde

Love is of all passions the strongest, for it attacks simultaneously
the head, the heart and the senses.
—Lao Tzu

As you walk through your sacred place you come to a room filled with light and color radiating from every corner and from above. When you enter, you touch the soft velvet textures of the fabrics surrounding you. Quiet, romantic music entices your senses to come alive, and your heart opens to connect with the beauty and depth of your Lover archetype. In this space you discover your ability to open your heart, express your feelings, activate your passion, and stoke the sexual fire at the core of who you are.

*O*ur Inner Lover is the most intimate, vulnerable part of who we are. She carries messages of love and connects with others by opening her heart. Lover connections are more than sexual connections; they encompass the ability to connect and love ourselves first, so we can connect and love others in an expansive way.

Characteristics of the Lover Archetype

Open Heart

Sensual

Loves Her Body

Sexual

The Lover Has an Open Heart

When our hearts are open, we want to connect deeply with others and we want to share our vulnerability. Intimacy is often defined as "into me see." To see and be seen requires opening up our hearts and becoming vulnerable. Intimacy is the willingness to see another person and allowing another to see us, which requires us to accept ourselves and another just as we are, without judgment.

When we listen from our hearts instead of our heads, we are magnetic and others want to be near us. When our hearts are open, we can sense how others are feeling. Our challenge is to listen without merging (heart too open) or detaching (heart closed). The Lover archetype allows us to keep our heart open and to listen without taking on the feelings or the pain of the one we are listening to. When we connect in this way, we are saying, "I want to hear what is going on with you and what you are feeling, and I can protect and love myself at the same time."

When we speak from our hearts, we are aware of the difference between our emotions and our feelings. Emotions are automatic responses that come from our archetypal depths. Feelings are our evaluation of these responses. Emotions are primitive, instinctual drives, and our feelings filter out what the body is experiencing and assigns a value to it and we communicate from that place. When we own our feelings and express them clearly, we can make a strong heart connection.

Often we project an image of a fairy-tale prince onto our partner, father, or friend and expect this person to wake us up, or search for us, or risk his life for us so we can be happy. The prince in fairy tales represents our inner masculine, not an actual male figure. We have within us both feminine and masculine aspects of the Lover archetype.

It is important to fall in love, not only with our femininity, but also to love the masculine part of ourselves. This has nothing to do with sexual preference; it is about becoming whole by acknowledging masculine and feminine Lover energy within us.

When we really know ourselves, our triggers, our ghosts of the past, our thoughts, our reactions, and the time when we can unite the masculine and feminine energies within ourselves, then we are safe to be with another.

When our hearts are open, we are able to be present to others by how we communicate with our body language. When we look into another's eyes, our eyes soften and we see beyond his or her face into the soul. Holding another in this way is giving them the space to be who they are, without judgments or conditions. When we are open, we allow others to see and support us as well.

A participant at a Woman Within Training shares her experience with her Lover energy:

The Lover archetype was amazing to me because I always

thought I had a wonderful intimate relationship with my husband, but when I came back from the training—I know this is going to sound strange—but it was the first time I really felt that my husband was holding me. It was the strangest experience, because I obviously knew he was holding me—but it was the first time I really got that it was me that he was holding! It was a whole new experience! Before, I could never have an orgasm unless I was imagining some kind of medical examination where no one cared about me. I always hated this sterile fantasy—now for the first time I could let that whole thing go and experience a whole new intimate relationship with my husband where I was a person and it was me he was holding and it was me as a person being cared about and loved that could have an orgasm! I enjoy being with my husband so much more now—as a human being who is loved! It's been an astounding shift for me.

Some of us may fall into the trap of giving ourselves away to others without loving ourselves. When we put all our energy into loving others without actively loving ourselves, we drain our life force and become an empty shell. Too much Lover archetypal energy leads to relationship addictions. One cause of this is not being nurtured as a child, and the only way we know to get nurturing is to give it to others, leaving us empty and feeling abandoned. When we give and get nothing in return, we tend to give more, thinking that someday we will feel loved. We will do anything to stay in connection in order to feel some semblance of love.

I fell into this trap on my wedding day. Many wedding ceremonies use the symbol of three candles to represent two people merging as one. When I got married, my husband and I lit the middle (unity) candle and then blew out our individual candles. This was symbolic of my belief that I had to give up myself and anticipate and fill my partner's every need before he asked. Instead of becoming a lover to my partner, I became his mother, and I lost all sense of who I was as an individual. A mother anticipates the needs of her child. A lover asks for what he or she wants. It took years to unravel this energy and reclaim my individuality so I could stop mothering my partner and become an equal lover. On our fortieth wedding anniversary, we did the ceremony again and relit our unity candle and kept our individual candles burning!

If women are enmeshed with others, they lose sight of themselves because they focus on others and lie to themselves about their own needs. Even if they are hit, beaten, or emotionally and physically abused, they are afraid to speak up for fear of losing the relationship. Domestic violence is a problem in our nation because many women do not love themselves first. They submit and do whatever is demanded of them. This may include engaging in sexual acts out of duty and obligation and not for pleasure and fulfillment. They cannot separate out who they are from who they think they are supposed to be. By staying enmeshed they feel lost, alone, and disconnected. Their hearts are too open to others and too closed to themselves. This results in low self-esteem and a belief that they have no right to be happy.

On the flip side, some of us may keep our hearts closed because somewhere in our pasts we learned that it hurt too much to keep our hearts open. If we close our hearts we are unable to connect deeply with others and end up feeling empty.

We attempt to fill up this void with addictions such as smoking, alcohol, drugs, sex, food, or work. When women are asked to describe what this feeling of emptiness looks like, they often characterize it as a black hole or a hole in the heart. When we acknowledge our addictions, we can then fill the void with love for ourselves and begin to open our hearts.

Marion Woodman, an expert of feminine psychology, describes what happens when addictions persist. In her book *Dancing in the Flames,* she says, "Addicts tend to develop a victim complex. Whether the source is a controlling parent or a physical or psychic trauma before, during, or after birth, they tend to experience themselves as born losers. 'Life,' 'the Universe,' everything is against them. In their powerlessness, they wonder where the next blow is coming from, or having given up wondering, they become defiant or resigned to accept whatever comes." If our relationships are not enhancing our growth, they are depleting our energy.

To change this pattern, we need to open our hearts and remember that we are lovable. We can be angry, fearful, playful, sad, or depressed and still be loved by others and, most of all, by ourselves. Sue, a participant at a Woman Within Training, is married to a successful engineer and has two healthy children. Her work felt hollow, and the problems at home seemed unending. Her husband struggles with chronic headaches and is unable to help with the children or around the house. Sue was becoming more and more depressed. Her connection with herself was missing.

As Sue told her life story, her pain was so deep she curled up into a ball on the floor. Between her sobs, she told us her mother died when she was very young and her father insisted she sleep with him and would fondle her. Because her father was lonely, Sue became his surrogate wife. As she spoke her shame and confusion, she felt heard and accepted for the first time, and she began to accept and love herself.

As she took in the feeling of being heard and accepted, Sue began to open her heart and fill her emptiness with the belief that she is lovable. Having been abandoned by her mother and then forced to be her father's lover, she had abandoned herself. As she felt supported and held, she learned to support and hold herself. Her mother was not there to do it and her father required her to love and hold him. Sue learned to trust others to hold, love, and accept her. By choosing to open her heart to others, she is able to open her heart and love herself.

Affirmations for an Open-Hearted Lover

- I listen to my heart and love myself.
- I open my heart to others and listen from my heart.
- I honor my masculine and feminine energies within me.
- I hold and am held with love.

The Lover Is Sensual

When we are aware of all our physical senses, our Lover archetype is alive. As we respond through increasing our sensitivity to odors, touch, taste, sight, and sound we awaken every cell of our bodies.

Awakening and activating our senses is exciting and invigorating. We fall in love with life when we look through the eyes of our Lover archetype. When we are touched by one who loves us, our skin radiates with light and energy. The feel of silk, velvet, linen, soft lamb's wool or cashmere on our skin brings us the ecstasy of sensuousness.

Smelling things we love—perfume, food, flowers, fresh-cut grass—can be as satisfying as being touched. The beauty of art, the furnishings in our homes, the way our loved ones look at us can envelop us in the arms of our Lover archetype. Listening to music we love, hearing the sound of our lover's voice creates physiological changes in our circulatory system as our heart beats faster and our hands sweat. When we fully taste food we love and let it linger on our tongues until every taste bud dances with joy, we experience the vastness of a sensual experience.

Take a moment to imagine a fine piece of chocolate. Look at its shape, its color, its size, any inscriptions or decorations. Now smell the chocolate and breathe in its rich aroma. Be aware of how the chocolate feels. Is it soft or hard? Is it melting, slowly conforming to the grooves of your fingerprint? Now put the chocolate into your mouth and let it slowly melt. Feel the sensations on your tongue as your taste buds come alive. Eating a piece of chocolate can be an orgasmic experience because all of your senses are activated. So it is with the Lover archetype.

The healthy Lover opens her heart and learns to listen to her body and her feelings to give her a complete experience of her world. Being sensuous allows us to be fluid and expansive. Allowing our breath to take in the fullness of each moment increases our pleasure of life and allows us to have fun and play with passion and joy.

When a woman is too sensual, she is lost in her senses and may do seductive, sexual things to get noticed and loved. She smothers those she loves and she demands to be touched, seen, and heard. Becoming too passionate causes disconnection instead of a healthy connection with another. The Lover archetype desires connection, yet when a woman tries desperately to get others to love her she experiences pain and distance from those she wants to love. She then becomes angry and resentful, and the result is chaos and drama in her relationships.

If we are driven by our senses, we may become addicted to that which brings us pleasure, such as food, cigarettes, shopping, alcohol, or sex. For example, smoking fills up our senses by the mesmerizing effect of smoke, taste, texture, odor. We are filled and satisfied for a moment, yet the senses need to be satisfied again and again.

If we become numb to our senses, we diminish our ability to have pleasure and passion in our life. One of the results of being depressed is shutting down the senses, which then shut down pleasure and passion. Instead of experiencing a sensual, full life, we feel numb and disconnect from our body and our heart. Life becomes boring and routine, and the richness and joy of life is lost.

Depression has reached epidemic proportion today and is the number one mental health disease of women. A woman who is depressed lacks enthusiasm and aliveness. She is bored and listless. She speaks in a monotone, and when asked, "What are you feeling?," she will typically answer, "I don't know" or "Fine." She may even dissociate from who she is and talk about herself in the third person, as if she is watching a movie. She has no sex drive and does not experience an orgasm when making love. She has no appetite, or she feels hungry and eats to fill up the void in her heart, not her stomach.

Some eating disorders are driven in part by seeking to find and fulfill the sensual Lover. Eating is one way to fulfill the senses, yet, when accomplished only through eating, comfort is obtained by continually wanting to experience the orgasm of food. She cannot separate out the desire for the sensual life that food offers with the desire of the Lover energy to connect with another. Her boundaries are very tight and closed, and she often finds herself feeling depressed, alone, and isolated.

There is a growing realization that many women have no pleasure during sex, no desire to have sex, and are suffering the psychological pain of lack of their sensuality. Our bodies are wired for pleasure, yet many women close down their connection to their senses, which causes their bodies and hearts to shut down.

Affirmations for a Sensual Lover

- I use all my senses to experience life.
- All of my senses are alive and active.
- I am fluid and expansive.
- My senses awaken my passion.

The Lover Is in Her Body

Our bodies are magical, marvelous creations of nature. Take a moment to consider the wonder and magic of your uterus, your breasts, your menstrual periods, your menopause, and your sexual response cycle.

It has been said that our bodies are temples for our feminine spirits. We each have special and unique bodies, and each one of us carries a magnetic presence that draws others to us.

When we love our body, we appreciate it and treat it with kindness. We take joy in adorning our bodies with clothes and jewelry that accentuate our figures in colors and styles that complement our beauty and make us feel good inside and out.

When we love our body, we listen to its signals. Our body tells us when it needs food, and it tells us when it is full. When we love our body, we choose healthy foods and know what foods serve and nourish us. Our body lets us know when we need rest and when we need to move. Our body tells us when we need to go to the bathroom.

When we love our body, we listen to it when it hurts and we do something to bring ease and comfort to it.

When we love our body, we treat it to massages, walks in nature, making love, decadent chocolate, or long leisurely baths.

When we love our body, we listen to its cues and clues of

distress. Our body's memories are accurate and hold volumes of information. Most women have not been taught how to listen to these messages from their bodies. Brenda Miller, author of *Season of the Body*, says, "The body knows a language the mind never wholly masters." Because of the depth of our body's wisdom, its distress is a message sent to us asking for attention.

When we love our body, we are *in* our body. We feel our feet on the floor, we move, stand, and walk with confidence, we are substance, and we love every moment of living.

When we love our body, we honor and bless our monthly period. Blood is the life force of the heart and as women; we are reminded monthly of this gift. Think back to the last time you had a period. Did you marvel at your body's ability to create a receiving blanket to receive a life and then shed this blanket so a new blanket could be woven in your uterus? Take time to listen to the messages your body is teaching you about life! Our body has the ability to grow new tissue and release an egg each month. If a sperm arrives, the miracle of creating life begins and if a sperm does not arrive, our womb is cleaned out and our body prepares the space again.

We can apply this Lover principle of preparing, waiting, shedding the old, and preparing again to many areas of our life. Are there relationships, ideas, work, and areas in our home where we are stuck in either preparing or waiting or shedding? We learn from our bodies how to prepare for receiving and creating new life.

When women are obsessed with their bodies, they lose sight of their hearts and create a disconnection with how their bodies affect others. It was a hot afternoon in July as men and women gathered for a conference on gender differences. A man with a staff and a woman holding two conch shells welcomed us. The man gave his welcome and greeting and then the woman invoked us to listen to her call to action. Her words paled as I looked at her body. She had on a long net dress covered with sequins over a spaghetti-strap short dress, three-inch spike heels, and her head wrapped in a serape, and I was struck by the difference between what I heard and what I saw. I was struck by the drama in her voice, and the words she spoke disturbed me. She spoke of how men in the world are raping women, yet nothing about how women are wounding men. Her purpose was to create connection between men and women, yet all I felt was seductiveness, drama, and disconnect from her and her message.

Some of the men's responses to this woman were "It was like she was in a glass cage—unapproachable and dangerous," "She was talking about the horrific rapes of women in the world, yet she was not aware of how she dressed affected me as a man." The most dissonant part was the message she *wanted* to get across as opposed to the way it was delivered. She had no idea that she was possessed by too much Lover archetypal energy and that her body spoke much louder than her words. Because of the way she was dressed, the audience was more taken by looking at her body than hearing the words she was delivering.

I have led hundreds of workshops for men and I am very aware of how my body can be a distraction for what I want to teach. My goal is not to dress down, but to dress in a way that does not draw attention to my body. My dress is very different if I am going out with my husband for an intimate evening. In this case, of course I want him to be attracted to me and my body.

When a woman obsesses about her body, she does whatever it takes to get love and attention. Drama becomes the mode for being seen and heard, and her real self is obscured by the drama. Every event is a drama that captures and engages all those around her.

This sometimes leads to promiscuity and she becomes a *femme fatale.* She may manipulate others by flaunting her body to prove her power as a woman. Instead of coming from a place where she accentuates her beauty and femininity, she takes away the mystery of her body and bares all. She is unconscious about the power of her body and uses her body to tease men and women. On the outside, it looks like she loves her body; however, she is usually miserable and hurting on the inside. She is so focused on how she looks that she is not aware of how others are responding to her.

When a woman hates her body and criticizes her beauty, she prostitutes herself. *Webster's* definition of the verb *prostitute* is "to corrupt or debase." So if we criticize ourselves or put ourselves down, we lose contact with our Lover archetype. The lack of love for our bodies threatens our ability to connect with others. Shame shuts us up. Love opens us up to connections with ourselves and others. Shame wraps its ugly fingers around our hearts and squeezes out our self-love. Sadly, many of us walk around hating our bodies.

We all carry the messages of not thin enough, too much hair, not enough hair, imperfect thighs, waist, lips … you name it. We perpetuate these messages for our young girls when we buy into these cultural messages from media and the patriarchal system.

Airbrushed and Photoshopped images of women in the media have created a false ideal of what we are supposed to look like. No wonder women struggle to measure up and feel shame for never being perfect enough. A psychological study in 1995 found that three minutes spent looking at a fashion magazine caused 70 percent of women to feel depressed, guilty, and shameful.

Women think they are supposed to have perfect bodies, which don't exist. So they focus on their imperfections and try to hide their bodies with clothes, makeup, hair dye, and a myriad of other commercial products for fear of being seen for who they really are.

Women struggle between showing their natural beauty and hiding behind masks.

Women who attend the Sexual Self Workshop offered by Woman Within International are asked to list shame-based messages growing up. Some of these are "Don't touch yourself down there," "Stifle the pleasure of masturbation," "All boys want is sex and it is up to us girls to control their sex drive," "Keep your body covered." These messages discourage us from enjoying the beauty of our bodies. As women wrestle with these cultural messages, their self-esteem suffers and they feel guilty if they attempt to go against what society has taught them. The good news is that we can rewrite these messages and form new ways of thinking to break free of the messages that tell us lies about ourselves and others.

If a woman hears herself say, "I am not good enough, not pretty enough, not dressed well enough," she continually compares herself to other women and can only see the beauty and talent in other women and fails to see her own beauty. As she measures herself against her internal messages and how she sees other women, she begins to hate herself, her body, and becomes jealous and vindictive toward herself and others.

Dee, a twenty-five-year-old woman, decided not to have children and had a hysterectomy to make sure that she wouldn't. She really wanted to like herself, yet every time she looked in the mirror, she hated her image. Her desire was to be more comfortable with her decisions and how she looks, so she signed up for a Woman Within Training. At the weekend, Dee shared with the other women that her conception was a surprise to her parents and they did not want a baby. She continued to suffer with the deep body belief that she was unwanted and a burden. To compensate for this, she tried to prove her worth by taking care of her mom, and she could not stand up for herself. In order to shift how she feels about herself, she looks into a mirror and imagines hearing positive messages from her "ideal" mom. These new messages are "I am so happy to have a beautiful little girl," "I am glad you were born," "You are perfect." As she breathed these messages into her body, she committed to write them on cards and tape them to her bathroom mirror so she could see them every day and take in the miracle of who she is. She now loves looking in the mirror and seeing her beauty.

The story of Snow White is a great example of how jealousy and lack of love for oneself can destroy a woman. Inside every woman is a Snow White, a beautiful princess. When she is ready to become a Queen, her critical messages (the evil queen) are activated and cause her to flee into the forest, where she lives with dwarfs. The dwarfs symbolize how she makes herself small and invisible instead of pursuing her right to be a Lover and a Queen. These messages continue to haunt her by tantalizing her with clothes, beauty products, and food, until she is finally consumed by these messages and falls asleep—or goes unconscious. The metaphor of sleep in fairy tales is about putting in our unconscious all that is true about us.

When we look in a mirror and fail to see our inner beauty, and instead see the Snow White in all the other women around us, we betray and deny space for our Lover archetype. We abandon ourselves by living with the dwarfed parts of ourselves instead of stepping into the beautiful women we are. For me, I look at pictures of myself when I was in my twenties and thirties and can't believe how beautiful I was then and didn't even know it!

What awakens Snow White is the masculine Lover energy in the form of a prince. This does not mean we need a man in our lives to wake us up. When we activate our inner masculine by *doing* something different to change our way of being, we can free ourselves from the curse of the negative messages. This active principle of the masculine calls us to redefine our messages and become visible in the world. Our Inner Prince is the doorway to becoming conscious, to wake us up, to enliven us, to call us to see the beauty and magnificence of our bodies.

Affirmations for a Lover in Her Body

- I love my body just the way it is.
- I listen to my body and heed its signals.
- I am grounded and present in my body.
- I bless the magic and magnificence of my body.

The Lover Is Sexual

Sexual energy is life-giving, connecting energy. We can learn to generate it, contain it, and use it to deepen and enrich our lives. The sacredness, the reverence, and the importance of being sexual are essential to our well-being. Learning how to feel safe with our sexual energy begins at birth and continues throughout life.

Accepting the sexual aspect of the Lover archetype opens us up to receive and to give love and pleasure. When the Lover archetype is used consciously in lovemaking, we regenerate ourselves and ignite the life force in our partner that connects to something larger than both of us.

Masturbation is a way to connect with our sexual energy to help us learn the art of making love with ourselves and then taking this learning into our sexual experience with our partners. Lovemaking does not come naturally; it takes practice and experimenting to discover what brings us pleasure and what stirs the fire of our passion within us from our toes to the top of our head. The raw instinctual erotic feelings of sexual desire need to be cultivated and understood so the bud of our sexuality can become an open beautiful flower.

Our sexual energy is not confined by our sexual preference or our age. Sexual energy is a primitive instinct that propels us to connect physically. We may have dreams about making love with the opposite sex as well as with the same sex. These dreams can be glorious and delightful, or they may confuse and scare us if we do not understand how the Lover archetype awakens us in our dreams so we can feel loved and connected through our sexual energy. It is important to accept the range of our sexual preference. Accepting this range deepens our Lover energy instead of restricting it. A healthy balanced woman accepts that she can feel sexual with men, with women, and with herself. One way to explore the possibilities our sexuality brings us is through the use of fantasies. Here's an example of a sexual fantasy:

> A woman is riding her horse through the forest and she comes upon a stream. She is drawn to the water, which is running cool and forming large pools among the moss-covered rocks. Her body is hot, so she dismantles her horse and tosses her long, flowing white dress over a rock. Through the branches, she sees a tall, handsome man looking at her with admiration and love. She pretends not to see him and slowly dips her toes into the water. Slowly, she lets the water take her in and it cools her skin, and she enjoys being watched. She massages her breasts and enjoys herself. She looks up and another woman is on the shore. This woman slowly takes off her dress and comes toward her. They embrace and play together as their nude bodies glisten in the sun. Their bodies tremble as they give and receive pleasure.

If a woman is obsessed with the sexual characteristic of the Lover archetype, she may give herself away to get attention and pleasure.

If she uses her body only as a sex object, she may need to close her heart in order to feel safe. Some women dress in ways that invite men and women to look at their bodies and not their hearts. They may unconsciously use their bodies to seduce others and then be left empty and alone when the result is only sexual gratification and the rest of the Lover characteristics are ignored.

Often sexual addiction becomes promiscuity. If we are not centered in who we are as whole women, we may use our seductive powers to draw others in. Our boundaries may be fuzzy and it is hard to say "No." We literally prostitute ourselves to be objects for others' pleasure, and although we may feel some pleasure, we still feel empty and restless and go on to the next affair or sexual encounter to find a meaningful connection. We are searching for the ultimate orgasm, the ultimate high, the filling of our holes.

Being obsessed with having enough sexual energy to keep our partners happy may cause us to have sex out of duty or obligation. We may have a compulsion to perform; however, the act is void of a spiritual connection and is only for sexual release or to keep our partner satisfied. Fear that our partner will leave if we do not perform our sexual duty keeps our Lover archetype locked up. Sometimes this obsession of looking for a sexual lover with whom we can feel more passion may lead us to have an affair in an attempt to reignite our passion.

Dorothy, a forty-five-year-old woman, a participant at a Woman Within Training, shared her story. She was molested at the age of nine; this was the first time she had shared this trauma with anyone. She has grown up unable to see her physical beauty and does not know how to love herself. She was addicted to sex because she connected getting love to having sex. However, when she had sex, she heard her perpetrator in her head saying, "Don't tell your mother."

"Your family will be ruined if you tell anyone." And "Doesn't this feel good?" Dorothy has let these messages silence her for thirty-six years and kept her from stating her needs or boundaries in any of her relationships. She longed to find her voice and talk about this long-held secret.

Through the use of role play, Dorothy faced someone playing the role of her perpetrator and she used her voice to express her anger and tell him how his actions have ruined her life. After she finished saying all she needed to say, she breathed a sigh of relief and looked around at the women who had witnessed her story and her anger. As she looked at the women her heart was filled with a deep blue color. She felt strong, warm, and lovable, and her face changed from being tense to a relaxed, happy smile.

For many women, sexual wounds from the past cause them to shut down their sexual energy altogether. A participant at a Woman Within Training shared how her sexual abuse blocked her Lover archetype. With tentative steps and noticeable shaking, Mary slowly took out the rumpled six-foot newsprint drawing of her body for all to see. Drawn in her abdomen is a caged dragon with fiery red eyes and sharp claws. Mary had not been sexual with her husband for two years, and her marriage held no passion. Her wild, sexual energy seemed dangerous; thus her desire to control this energy has drained her sexual passion. When she was a teenager, her father would slip into her room at night and lie down next to her, caress her, and in the name of "love" fondle and kiss her, which, for all she knew, was normal love between a father and daughter. His words confused her: "Don't ever tell anyone about this special time between the two of us." And so she grew up with a secret, represented as a caged dragon inside her womb that kept her Lover archetype caged and safe.

Mary drew these feelings as an animal with claws, representing her need for self-protection and symbolizing the destruction of her abuse. Fear of her sexual desires kept her Lover energy caged and trapped in her body. This trapped energy made her sick and poisoned her body and all her relationships. She became frigid and suppressed her sexual feelings and desires. Because of the incest, she had made a decision to close the door to her heart and her body. In order to free the caged dragon, Mary became the dragon and faced her father in a metaphoric process. In this process another woman stepped into the role of her father and through psychodrama allowed Mary the opportunity to express to her father her rage and fear. She awakened her Lover energy and created a new pathway to her sexuality and her heart. By freeing her dragon, she reconnected with her pure Lover energy.

When sexual energy is denied or repressed, the result is often emptiness and fear. Often there are many layers of sexual shame. Religious and cultural messages stop us from feeling free to be sexual. Our sexual desire shuts down and goes into the dungeon of our sacred place, where it hides until we feel safe enough to explore the ramifications of our shame and free our desires once again.

Affirmations for a Sexual Lover

- I accept and express my sexual energy.
- I explore how to pleasure myself and allow myself to be pleasured.
- I am open to the range of my sexual experiences.
- I use sexual fantasies to invigorate my sexual experience.

Questions and Exercises to Discover Your Lover Archetype
Take a deep breath, close your eyes, and visualize your Inner Lover. Take in another deep breath and describe the odors that waft around

you. Do these odors stimulate pleasant memories, or do they create discomfort in your body? Keep breathing. Focus now on the image of yourself as a lover. Imagine what you look like, say and do when you fully embraced your Lover archetype. Imagine yourself totally in love with your body and see how love radiates from your eyes and every pore of your skin. See this image of yourself. Are you clothed or naked? Is the image close or far away? Does this image of your Lover speak to you? If so, what does she say? Do you know this part of yourself? Do you want to get to know her better? What colors surround you? Is anyone else in your image with you? What sounds or words do you hear from your Inner Lover? What are you feeling about yourself as you get acquainted with this archetype of yourself? Is she just about sex and sensuality or does she emanate warmth and connection? Take a moment to journal your experience of what you see, hear, smell, feel, touch, and taste. Be aware of what is happening in your body as you explore this part of yourself.

Take time to have a love affair with your body. Go to a mirror and look into your eyes and say, "I love you." Affirm the beauty of who you are. If the daily messages you tell yourself are negative, rewrite them.

Write a love letter to yourself from your Lover archetype. Let yourself hear all the compliments and affirmations your soul yearns to hear from someone else. Be aware of how you love yourself and find ways to create a loving connection with yourself.

Learn the value of sexual fantasies. Write in your journal a favorite sexual fantasy.

Take some time to identify what or who may still be keeping you from opening your heart. The question you need to ask is, "What or who caused me to close my heart to myself and others?"

When you are struggling with a relationship, ask yourself the following questions: "Is this a connection that is important to me? Am I connected to this person for the wrong reasons? Is this connection serving me or draining me?"

Be aware of how you dress and what you are communicating to others through how you present yourself.

Take a moment to list messages about your sexuality, and then convert any negative ones into positive messages. For example, the message, "Keep your body covered." can be rewritten to "My body is beautiful and touchable and lovely to look at."

Look at yourself in a mirror and touch yourself. What areas are sensitive and respond to your touch? What areas do not feel good being touched? Since your skin is your largest sex organ, getting to know the lay of the land will increase your pleasure. Mapping all the places in your body that can bring you pleasure also begins the process of sexual healing.

Paula Alter's Story

As a management consultant, over the years I have been in many meetings and training sessions. Establishing a strong relationship with my clients is crucial to being able to do my job well. I love it when that happens naturally and easily. Occasionally I meet someone whom I can't seem to connect to.

I recognized that my ability to create relationships is one of my strengths and is based in my appreciation of people and wanting the best for them. Archetypically I would say that was my "Lover energy" expressing itself.

What I found difficult was when I couldn't connect. Whether it was me or them, I found it confusing and ultimately affected my ability to work well with that person. I would either go into self-criticism or try to find ways to "seduce" them into liking me. Not sexual seduction, but jokey chat, or participating in surface-level conversation for too long, essentially being ineffective.

After one such meeting I had a light bulb moment. This was a meeting with a new client and I was experiencing difficulty in establishing the kind of relationship where we could get to what was important to be addressed. I felt diminished and not in my power at all.

In exploring the Lover archetype I could see that where I went in situations like this was too much lover. In that particular meeting what would have been more balanced was to bring up my light Warrior energy, to meet this person where he was rather than focusing on trying to feel comfortable any way that I could.

I've since used this awareness to notice when "too much Lover" is present and to shift my energy to what is needed. I have learned that I have a wide range of ways to be that serve both my clients and me.

Chapter 7

Invite Mother to Birth and Sustain Your Creations

Creation is continuous.
—Native American proverb

All the principles of heaven and earth are living inside you.
Life itself is truth, and this will never change.
Everything in heaven and earth breathes.
Breath is the thread that ties creation together.
—Morihei Ueshiba

Your journey through your sacred place continues as you enter a large room that looks like a chemical laboratory or a kitchen. This is the place where common substances, usually of little value by themselves, are used to create something of great value. This is the place of your Mother Within. A place where you can honor, nurture, teach, sustain, and heal all of your creations that you bring forth from within you. As you mix together all of your life experiences—your hurts and your joys—your mission and purpose of what you want to create becomes clear.

*I*t is easy to take the Mother archetype for granted because it is so much a part of our nature as women. Psychologists and therapists spend hours helping us sort out the effects and issues surrounding the mother who birthed or raised us as well as how our own mother instincts shape us every day. Often it is through our childhood experiences with our mother that we can see the value and impact of the Mother archetype in our life. As we call in our Mother archetype, we gain her power and gifts.

Our Inner Mother nurtures, teaches, sustains, protects, and heals us. By tapping into the universal archetypal Mother energy, we learn about Mother, the source of all creation. Carl Jung calls the maternal instinct the mysterious root of all growth and change. Just like a plant, the root goes down into Mother Earth and gets it nutrients so it can grow into its potential.

The word *mother* is a noun and a verb. When used as a noun, it refers to a person charged with energy necessary for our life. When used as a verb, it refers to behaviors she uses to support and sustain life.

How we see ourselves as mothers and how we relate to our own mothers affects all of our creations. These creations may be children, businesses, gardens, books. If we have a strained or distant relationship with our mother, we may be hesitant to examine how this relationship affects us. If we have a close relationship with our mother, we may be more accepting of our Mother archetypal energy.

Women tend to project their unaccepted Mother traits onto their birth or childhood mothers or other women in their lives. When we are conscious of these projections, we can own the Mother archetypal traits that we do not like and transform them in ways that can serve us and others. When we accept our Mother archetype as a part of us, we accept the vital part of our nature as women.

In order to balance the aspects of our positive and negative Mother energy, it is necessary to examine the characteristics of Mother and see how we use them to birth and sustain our creations.

> ### Characteristics of the Mother Archetype
>
> Creates
>
> Nurtures
>
> Teaches
>
> Heals

The Mother Creates

Women are the creators of life. When we accept our Mother archetype we accept our goddess-like ability to give life. Knowing this part of ourselves quickens our womb and reconnects us with our purpose for living. Our womb is like a pot in which alchemical processes take place to magically transform one substance into something else. For example, when we cook, we combine many different ingredients to create a meal that is nutritious and reflects our unique ability to combine substances. This is not unlike creating a quilt, which uses scrap pieces of old clothing to create a piece of art, or mixing paint on a canvas to create a picture. All creations take our life experiences, our dreams, and our desires to transmute them into something through which we can live our mission.

Page Rossiter, a Woman Within facilitator, shares her story of how she has used the creative aspect of Mother in her life:

> I always hoped that one day I would wake up and desire children with all of my being. That day has yet to happen. Now, while most of my friends are mothers, I am choosing to not have children. I know this to be a good choice for me,

my husband, and our life together. I also know that I will miss some unique experiences: carrying a baby in my womb, the joys and tribulations of breast feeding a newborn, and the intricacies of watching my offspring grow up. A small part of me will always wonder and grieve the choice, even though it feels right in my bones. Due to this, I have been keenly attracted to uncovering how my archetypal Mother energy is expressed. What I discovered is a multitude of other areas that are rich and innate; it is the tapestry that is my life.

For many years I was involved in leading youth camps that promoted community amongst diverse populations. The program was intense and emotional for everyone involved. It was a natural place for my archetypal Mother energy to show up. I loved watching these teenagers experience breakthroughs, while learning from and connecting with one another. Several teens asked if I would adopt them … and in my heart, I did.

My biggest creation is the ever and continually changing me. I hold the awesome responsibility, power, and the choices to create my life each day. With every new experience I give birth to another part of myself. What a gift. What a joy!

Within our minds and hearts are millions of seeds that contain the potential of creation. Once the seed is planted, we are changed in every way: physically, emotionally, and spiritually. The creator part of us is responsible for incubating and maturing each of these seeds. Whether we have an idea, a yearning, or an embryo growing in our womb, we are all mothers. In order to give birth, it is necessary to grow up and be ready for this responsibility. When we are pregnant with an idea or a child, our bodies and minds belong to our creation. We make choices to support our creations so they can grow.

When my daughters-in-law were pregnant, I watched how they provided nurturing for new life by making different food choices, activity choices, and preparing a new space. As I watched them, I wondered, "What seed is growing inside of me?" I have planted many seeds of ideas throughout the years. I have many ideas for books, for articles, for workshops. If I spend time planning and preparing for the creative seeds inside of me, I will be amazed what I can give birth to.

Everything we create becomes a part of us for the rest of our lives. For example, after a child is born, fetal cells continue to circulate in a woman's body. What we give birth to circulates forever in future generations. The act of creation is a sacred act. Cooking, teaching, sewing, gardening, and writing are all examples of sacred acts that require us to remember our breath and the importance of breathing life into our creations.

As part of my writing journey, I had a fantasy that some magical energy would enter my body, move my pen, create words, and my book would be done. I learned that creating—just like a baby in a mother's womb—required all of me: my mind, my body, my emotions, my spirit. "I want to be inspired to write," I shout. "I am not inspired!" The word *inspire* means "to breathe." To create I must breathe! By breathing, I open myself to what is coming into my thoughts, my heart, and my pen. When I breathe I release the tension that holds my body tight, and my creative energy is freed. In all creation it is important and necessary for a mother to breathe in order to give birth.

Gayle, fifty-one, has searched for her creative spirit for the past twenty years. She worked for her husband's company, which went bankrupt and left Gayle lost as to what she wanted to do with her creative energy. Her focus had been on her husband for so long that she did not know what she wanted to do, and she was terrified of failing. At a Woman Within Training, she discovered her Mother Within and realized she could nurture her own Infant self and be open to see and accept her gifts and talents. She started a journal about what she loves to do, and she connected with her magical Child and her childhood dreams to get ideas of where to begin. As a result of this process, Gayle created a successful clothing design business that is flourishing.

The creative part of Mother has a side of her that also destroys in order to create. Just as Kali, the Hindu goddess of creation, symbolizes giving birth and destruction, the Mother archetype is just as capable of destroying as she is of creating. Mother Nature, our Earth, is a great example of what happens when too much creative energy dominates. When the forest becomes densely populated, the saplings die. Too much rain kills crops. The proliferation of wolves kills off the moose population. Weeds choke out vegetation needed for food. Floods, volcanoes, tsunamis, earthquakes are all examples of the destructive nature of Mother Nature.

It is painful and difficult to accept that we have within us a need to destroy what we have created. Sometimes we may become so frustrated, depressed, or overwhelmed that the thought of destroying our creations rumbles through our minds. Ignoring or repressing these thoughts is dangerous and harmful. Recognizing and acknowledging that these thoughts are a natural part of the creative process makes us safe and puts us in charge of our Mother energy. We then know we can call on other archetypal energies to help us manage these thoughts and feelings when they arise.

Any woman who has planted flowers and tended a garden knows

that in order for her garden to flourish she needs to destroy the weeds and thin out the growth. This is true for any of our creations. In business, it is often necessary to cut back, prune, and make way for new growth, just as pruning a plant makes it healthier and stronger. For many women, using this skill of the Mother is difficult. As women, we tend to form deep connections with our employees, so when the time comes to reorganize companies, letting some of the employees go, we may feel great distress—yet the need to change creates the need to destroy what was.

If a leader of an organization or business has too much creator energy, she can choke out the vitality of the organization by micromanaging and controlling others. Others feel devoured by her and are unable to move and grow. If this happens, she becomes the victim of what she created.

If we have too much creative energy, our world becomes chaotic and we may feel unfocused, confused, stressed out, and torn in many different directions. We may feel burned out. Perfection and jealously often accompany this drive to produce, and we may give birth to more than we have the energy to nurture and sustain.

When the Mother inside of us is focused on surviving, we may have very little energy to tap into our creative spirit. Feeling paralyzed is a common result of too little creative energy. We may have loads of ideas, creative thoughts, and desires and yet never bring them to fruition because they stay in the embryonic state. We may be a fantastic generator of ideas and yet be unable to follow through. We may have an idea and let it incubate for years waiting until we have enough time, enough energy, and enough money to give the idea birth. Waiting destroys ideas.

The availability of birth control and abortion has given women control of their biological life-giving power. Yet many women use "psychological birth control" to stop the creative forces in their lives. Because of work, being too busy, or lacking confidence—whatever the "pill"—our ideas are not given a chance to gestate and be birthed.

Some women fail to create because they feel overwhelmed by all the changes that they need to make in order to bring something new to life. A woman may resent having to make changes, or if pregnant with a child, may resent the changes in her body. A woman who wants to plant a garden may dream about what it will look like as she browses through the websites and catalogs looking at all the possible flowers she can plant, however, she may loathe giving up her days off to work in the blistering sun to plant the seeds so she can enjoy her creation. Building a business requires sacrifices of money, time, and energy, and if fear takes over the creative energy stays buried, the business will not be birthed.

Ann is a divorced woman who deeply desired a relationship with a man. However, she was paralyzed in her ability to find creative ways to meet a man, and she did not take the time to explore creative ways to make herself visible and available. For some time she stayed bitter and alone, waiting for some magical godmother to appear and take her to the castle to meet her prince. Yet once she took the step to sign up for a dating service, she began to see possibilities of giving birth to a new relationship.

One thing that stops our creative energy is comparing our ideas to others. Because we feel less than, we experience angst and conflict that paralyzes and destroys our creative spirits. By comparing ourselves to others, we forget that we are unique with a special gift to offer that may look similar to another's gift—yet it cannot be the same because of who we are. We tend to minimize our creativity because of so many messages from our past that discourage us from letting ourselves be visible and heard.

When we cut off or close down our creative energy, we tend to isolate and become depressed. If we want to bring something to life, whether it is an idea, a business, a book, or a new relationship, yet we don't take time to incubate the idea or project, our creative Mother energy goes underground. Our ideas are aborted because we do not give energy to their growth.

A woman who has had an abortion, whether it was the loss of a child or an idea that was cut short, needs to grieve the loss. If the loss is repressed and shoved down into the unconscious, feelings may surface to threaten her ability to birth new creations. Perhaps others forced her to make the choice of aborting her child or idea. To find peace, she needs to face the conflict this choice created inside of her and say good-bye to the loss in order to release the energy from her body.

When we are paralyzed by a past hurt or failure, we need to take the time to acknowledge the experience and release the hurt and pain. When I was in college, my sociology professor made a comment on a paper I wrote—"A good try that didn't quite come off"—that kept me paralyzed for years. By reworking that message, I came up with a new message: "Your creations are worth your energy and bless the world."

Affirmations for a Creating Mother

• I am bringing newness to the world.

• I support my creative ideas so they can be birthed.

• I breathe life into my creations.

The Mother Nurtures

Once our idea or child is birthed, the task is to nurture this fragile bud so it can blossom in its own way. This requires the mother to provide warmth, food, and shelter to sustain her creation. We not only nurture children, we nurture relationships, our careers, our hobbies, and all that we invest our life energy into.

From the moment of inception, a mother nurtures her creation so it can survive and thrive. This requires her to be attuned to what feels nurturing to her creation, which may be very different than what she thinks her creation needs. For example, I love plants in my home. To nurture and sustain them, I attune to each plant's need for water, light, and food. If I do not do this, I destroy my plants by overwatering them or not watering them enough.

An important ingredient in nurturing our creation is learning to nurture ourselves. If we did not receive this nurturing as a child, we need to find ways to learn to nurture ourselves. Often we can get this nurturing from close women friends, sometimes a grandmother or aunt. The danger some women face is trying to find this kind of nurturing from a male partner. Romantic nurturing is very different than Mother nurturing.

Take a look at the word *smothering* and see the word hidden inside. When the word *mother* is removed, the word left is *sing*. Too much nurturing energy keeps our creation from singing. Our creation sings when we back away and allow it to evolve. A smothering Mother takes the life out of her creation because she does not allow it to breathe or sing its own song.

Smothering is like overwatering plants, forcing a toddler to eat, or holding on to a book or poem we write because we are afraid to be exposed. Smothering can be construed as "I love you so much I want you to eat," or "I love you so much I don't want you to get hurt." This communicates that the Mother is the powerful all-knowing one and the creation is weak. To counter this, we need to empower our creation to learn, even if it means watching our creations suffer in order for them to change and grow.

When Mother energy nurtures her creation too much, she devours its essence through her overvigilance.

In the spring Mallard ducks come to our pond in Michigan. In my need to nurture and sustain them, I feed them every day. I call out, "Where are my babies?," and the ducks come running up to my door. I love being the source of their food, and the ducks love to be fed. When winter sets in, the pond freezes, and I continue to call for "my babies," and they continue to come. My kind nurturance and my need to feel like a powerful nurturer becomes smothering love that kills these "babies." Instead of following their instinct to migrate, the ducks rely on me to provide their food, and in this reliance, they die from the cold. In the movie, *As Good as It Gets,* Helen Hunt, playing the role of the waitress, says, "I hug my son more than he wants *because I need it.*"

Even after my sons were grown I still wanted to control and nurture them by giving them money and gifts. I wanted to be needed and loved, so giving them money was a manipulative way to hold on. When our oldest son went to college, we had an agreement that he would pay for his tuition. I felt the pain of him having to find enough money to live and pay his tuition. I knew I had to let go, yet I would mail him a check, slip a $20 bill in his pocket, or continue to buy him clothes. The more adamant my husband got about not giving him any money, the more I needed to do so.

One day my son came home and said, "I don't want you to do anything for me. I don't want you to buy me clothes, write me, and call me. I need to break free from you. I need to figure out how to grow up and I need to do it by myself." Of course I was panic-stricken, thinking I was never going to hear from him again. He needed time to find out who he was apart from me, and he needed to prove that he could do it himself. I realized that my son was no longer a dependent little boy—he was a man I was proud of who wanted to stand on his own two feet.

When my younger son was seventeen years old, he went to Europe for a year. In his final preparations, I accompanied him to an American Express office, where he applied for a credit card. He was turned down, so I begged and pleaded with him to let me write him in on my card, and he could take that in case he needed cash for an emergency. It was the nurturing, devouring mother at work. My son turned to me and said firmly, "No, Mom, I don't want your card. I want to do this myself and I want you to leave me alone." The feelings that welled up in me were sadness and pride. I was sad that I could no longer use my nurturer to help, and pride because I saw a man who could nurture himself, not a needy little boy.

If we do not let go of our creations and continue to hang on with desperation, they become depleted and dependent. Instead, it is important to bless our creations and let them go.

The problem lies in the paradox. What looks and seems loving may be very destructive. Motherhood can be like an octopus. Once this energy gets its tentacles around a possession, it chokes out its life. Whether it is an animal, a child, or a project, our Mother tentacles reach out, surround, and encompass. When we become conscious of this tendency, we can release our grip and provide healthy nurturing.

I sat across the table from a vital, forty-year-old successful businesswoman. In our process of getting to know each other, I asked if she had children. Quick to reply, she said, "Yes, I have three. They are eight, fourteen, and forty-one." I must have looked puzzled with her response, because she quickly added, "Oh, the forty-one-year-old is my husband." Trying not to gasp, I felt my stomach cramp. By seeing her husband as a child, she is unconsciously destroying him and their relationship. The danger of this archetype flares when women mother their partners. Many women fall into this trap because many men did not receive positive nurturing from their mothers, and they look to their partners to fill this void. This works for a while; however, the relationship begins to erode and the scales tip. What was once a nurturing, loving behavior becomes a critical, shame-filled message; the woman needs to be in relationship with a grown man, not a little boy seeking to be nurtured by his mother.

Fathers are often deeply affected by the birth of their children. They may withdraw and resent this new creation because they observe their partner giving the infant the nurturing they wished they had received. A man can never understand the depth of connection that a woman has to her child. If we pay too much attention to our creations and neglect our partners, we may damage our relationships. It is easy for a mother to give all of herself over to her creation and forget about others. This can happen with a business, a career, a hobby, and volunteer work, as well as a child.

On the other end of smothering our creations is the tendency to withhold nurturing because we feel we have nothing to give. After giving birth, some mothers feel depressed, inadequate, lonely, and overwhelmed. When this happens, these feelings cause a survival mechanism to be activated to protect herself, often by sleeping or crying, disappearing, drinking, or hiding. We cannot nurture another when we feel depleted.

Judy was sexually abused by her therapist, and because of this traumatic experience, she lost her sense of purpose. Although she has a doctoral degree, she didn't know what she wanted to do with her life. Her energy and creativity were diminished, and she did not know how to nurture herself. She wanted to increase her physical fitness and vitality and focus less on others and more on herself. At a Woman Within Training she realized how much she needed to be nurtured, so she asked another woman she felt safe with to hold her and sing to her. As she was held, she could feel her heart open and she closed her eyes and got an image of holding and loving her Inner Child who had not received the nurturing she needed.

We may withhold nurturing from our creations because we never learned how to nurture. Many women have never been held and nurtured by a woman in ways they need or want. We, as woman, are looked to as the nurturers of the world, yet in order to be nurturing, we need to be nurtured.

Jamie is a fifteen-year-old girl with long blonde hair, deep blue eyes, and sunken cheeks who was deprived of touch and nurturing. Jamie dealt with this lack of love by not eating and became anorexic. Through much internal searching, she realized that she deserves to be nurtured; she began to ask for touch from other women and she is learning how to love and nurture herself in all ways—emotionally, spiritually, intellectually, and physically.

Affirmations for a Nurturing Mother

- I nurture myself so I can nurture others.
- I know the boundaries of my nurturing energy.
- I let my creations sing.

The Mother Teaches

Teaching is an inherent part of the Mother archetype. In order for our creations to become all they are meant to be, they need discipline, guidance, and instruction. Whether the teaching is done from a conscious place of "Today, I am going to teach my employees about customer service," or from an unconscious place of modeling our values and beliefs through our behaviors and what we say, we are teachers. When teaching comes from an unconscious place, it is usually from behaviors we learned from Mother figures in our lives that we pass on to our creations.

Mothers have a special wisdom to share with their creations. The owl on the shoulder of Athena, the goddess of wisdom, is a symbol of female intelligence and a sense of Mother intuition that is all-seeing. When we let our Inner Mother teach us about ourselves, we can unlock places in our unconscious that enlighten us and help us and our creations. By spinning information and experience together we fortify and strengthen our creations through our teachings.

My mother taught me that people are very important and unique. She taught me to love people of every color and creed. She invited people from all over the world into our home. My mother loved the diversity of people, and because of this tapestry, I set my goal to go to Africa as a nurse. Although I did not go to Africa, my creation of Woman Within has touched the lives of many women in many parts of the world.

As teachers we are sensitive to and see the potential in our creations. We then provide opportunities for growth. Often, this may be through letting our creations experience the natural consequences of their behavior instead of lecturing and preaching to them. How we teach our creations makes an everlasting impact on what we created.

If the teacher is focused on her personal goals and not on the goals of her creation, the result is criticism, judgment, and shaming. This causes her creation to shrink and exist only to please mother. Often, criticism is seen as a gift to make something or someone better. It is important to deliver constructive feedback in an empowering way so the creation can improve; however, criticism can be disempowering. The way the message is delivered affects our student-creation.

After a Woman Within weekend, I gave feedback to a facilitator about how she dressed. Her clothes were wrinkled and her slacks were stained and not hemmed. I gave her factual, clear feedback in front of her peers, which was hurtful to her. She felt shamed and embarrassed. In this example, I used critical teacher energy, and as a result I damaged our relationship.

How could I have been an empowering teacher? First, I became aware that I was asking her to fit into my standard of dress. Second, if her dress presented an unprofessional image for the program, then I needed to speak to her in private about her image and its effect on me and how I judged that her image affected the participants. Then we could come to some mutual understanding of what might work and both be empowered.

By criticizing others and ourselves, we struggle to feel okay about ourselves. Underneath our critic is a desire to be the best person possible. Teaching too much can also turn into shaming. When this happens, the creation feels, "I am not good enough" or "I am defective." Mary and John have been in a relationship for three years. Mary began to realize how much she shames John by commenting on everything he does that doesn't measure up to her standards—from the way he dresses, the way he relates to their children, to how he responds or doesn't respond to her needs. When John hears these shaming messages, he becomes small and invisible and Mary becomes his shaming Mother.

What can Mary do differently? She can nurture the differences between her and John, let go of her high expectations, and accept John as he is. By tapping into her Queen energy and treating him like a King she can diffuse this destructive shaming energy in her relationship and transform it to empower them both.

Shame messages can be delivered through a look, a touch, a side comment, a sarcastic remark. If our mothers constantly criticized us, we may feel flawed and feel like something is wrong with us. As we discern the difference between "we did something bad" and "we are bad," we can change the messages in our heads to empower us instead of destroying us. Instead of saying to ourselves, "I am a horrible person," we can say, "Oops, I made a mistake and I can learn from my mistakes." When we hide our true selves for fear of being shamed, then shame covers our essence.

If we deny our ability to teach what we know, our creation does not benefit from our knowledge and guidance, and we end up abandoning our creations. One way this shows up is how we teach our children about sex and their changing bodies. The omission of teaching about sex creates confusion and secrecy in the child. The child is then left to figure out what sex is all about.

A positive example of how parents can teach their children about sex is provided by Laurie and Rich, who have three beautiful daughters, ages nine, fourteen, and fifteen. On each daughter's ninth birthday, they took her out for a special dinner where she was celebrated. Laurie and Rich talked to her about how her body was changing and answered her questions about sex. Each daughter learned that she has permission to talk about sex to both of her parents, and she gets both the female and the male perspectives. What Laurie and Rich learned is that each daughter had a different reaction to this experience, and they were able to incorporate each daughter's unique response into dealing with other sensitive subjects as they came up.

In the area of relationships, we abandon our partner if we expect our partner to figure out and fill our needs instead of teaching our partner what we need. Expecting our partner to figure out and fill our needs is destructive to our relationships. The same goes for the creation of a business, a project, or a book. In order for our great ideas to flourish, we need to ask for what we need.

Affirmations for a Teaching Mother

- I weave my experiences and information to teach others.
- I honor my Mother wisdom and use it to support my creations.
- I see the potential in my creation and provide opportunities for growth.

The Mother Heals

Mother has the ability to heal her creation through her touch, her look, her thoughts and prayers. By recognizing and accepting this gift, we can use it in meaningful ways to change ourselves and others for the better. The healing energy of Mother is magical and has the power to change and renew her creation. This can look like kissing a "boo-boo" or holding our creation in our thoughts and sending loving positive thoughts to our grown children, our gardens, or the employees of our business. We heal when we listen to our creation.

Healing means making whole, and the Mother archetype leads people to a place of magical transformation. I had the wonderful experience of being held by Amma, the Hugging Saint and revered Mother from India. As I crawled into her lap and felt her arms around me, my body melted into hers, and I felt the blessing and healing coming from her heart into my heart. Deep sobs came from inside my soul, and as Amma wiped away my tears, I experienced the profound connection to knowing myself anew.

We can use Mother healing energy to heal ourselves. The next time you are feeling low or out of sorts, check in with yourself and ask how old you feel. Then imagine your healing Mother inside of you holding and comforting this young part of yourself.

As an adult woman I often visit my parents in my hometown. As was customary in my family, we go to church on Sunday morning. On one occasion, as I sat in church, I remembered how all the "young" parts of me hated sitting still in church. During the service, I spent time healing these young parts of me. I accessed my Inner Mother and imagined my anxious five-year-old in my arms. I affirmed her dislike of sitting still and alone during church and told her that it was okay to want to run and play. I also visualized my Adolescent and told her she could go to the local café and hang out with her friends and I would pick her up after church. This image calmed me and healed my past hurts around being forced to go to church as a child and adolescent.

If we were forced to become the caretakers (healers) of our parents when we were young, we may struggle to accept our ability to heal others. For example, Karen's father was an alcoholic and her mother suffered from depression and anxiety. Karen did not receive support or involvement from them; instead she was the adult and took care of her parents. In addition, she had an emotionally disturbed sister who was extremely abusive physically, mentally, and verbally. Karen felt a lot of anger at her parents for not protecting her from her sister. Because all she knew was how to be a caretaker, she attracted people who wanted to be taken care of. Also, she lost her voice and couldn't communicate her wants or needs.

At a Woman Within Training, Karen discovered how to access the healing characteristic of her Mother archetype. First, she needed to call in her Warrior archetype and release her anger and set healthy boundaries. Then she needed to heal her heart by finding ways to get nurturing and rebuild trust in others.

Nancy, a thirty-year-old single woman, had a strained relationship with her hypercritical mother. She found her mother's nervous energy so annoying and hurtful to be around that she would often lose her temper at her mother. Yet she saw how she criticizes others, just like her mother, and she wants to change this pattern and tap into her healing Mother energy.

When Nancy worked on this issue at a Woman Within Training, she began to feel pain in her hip. As she explored this pain, she remembered that she was emotionally and sexually abused by her father when she was six years old. As she sank into this memory, her heart began to heal her six-year-old self by listening to her fear and holding her and telling her she is safe with the woman within Nancy. As Nancy imagined her six-year-old being nurtured and healed, the pain in her hip disappeared and a rich red feeling surrounded her body as she reclaimed her ability to heal herself.

When we use our Mother energy to heal ourselves, we are then available to be present so our creations can heal where they hurt. When my children were little, I provided an environment to support their psychological and physical healing. They were responsible for their own healing, yet my Mother energy could be creative in offering suggestions and seeing beyond the obvious. My sons are now adults, and my Mother energy extends out to them to "hold" them in my thoughts when they are going through a painful time. I imagine angels hovering around them and healing their pain or giving them courage to go through a difficult situation. Another thing I do is light a candle to send healing light to them.

The Mother archetype heals when she listens to her creation. Our ability to tune in to what we have created is a way to discover where we need to be present and where we need to back off and give our creation some space in order for it to heal.

Too much healer can appear as loving and caring at first; however, the intention may be just the opposite. Many fairy tales associate the archetypal Mother image with an evil, destructive, toxic stepmother. In the Snow White fairy tale, the witch brings items to entice Snow White's beauty (comb and corset) and to nourish her (an apple). Each gift is presented as a loving thing; however, each gift is poisonous. Too much healer can appear as loving and caring at first, however, the intention may be just the opposite. The effects of this poisonous behavior are usually invisible and insidious. It does its destructive work in secret. The witch uses toxic love for her selfish purposes. The witch mother seeks to destroy in others what has been destroyed in her. The effects of this poisonous behavior are usually invisible and insidious. It does its destructive work in secret.

If we use our magical skills to bring toxicity to our creations, the power benefits us, not our creation. At the Mother's Shadow workshop I lead for men, I hear many men speak about their confusion between love and control. Men continue to let their mothers control them in order to get a morsel of love. Mothers use their martyr and victim behaviors to coerce and keep the sons guilty and small. Just as the witch in Hansel and Gretel seems kind, with the intent to heal and strengthen the children, her intent is for her own nourishment. At first the children feel loved and nourished and begin to get healthy. How confusing for them when they realize they were intended as food for the witch. In order to get free from the deceptive healer, they use their own cleverness to overtake this energy. There are many healers caught up in their grandiosity and living from their need to feel powerful and special.

Creating a beautiful home is something many women do well. It is not enough to decorate, bring in flowers, and rearrange the furniture. For a home to thrive, it needs to be infused with our healing energy. This is energy that can be sensed, not necessarily seen. When we walk into a room and feel peace and serenity, then we know that it has been infused with healing energy. One way this is accomplished is through meditating or praying in your home. Our animals and pets respond to this kind of energy too. When I travel a lot and am away from my home, my home suffers from my absence. Not only does the dust accumulate, but there is a lack of lightness, freedom, and clarity. The fountain has run dry; the flowers that were on the table have wilted. The refrigerator is bare and our cat is constantly crying to let us know that he is not at all happy with us being gone. My home environment needs my healing energy as much as the people I serve on my travels.

Owning our power to heal is the first step in making a difference. The next step is to take responsibility to share our healing gift with others. When we seek healing for ourselves, we can radiate healing energy to others. Many of the women who have trained to become facilitators of the Woman Within process have established their own healing practices, from counseling to massage therapy, Reiki, parenting classes, and so on. One facilitator, who was going to school to be a lawyer saw her healing potential once she had healed a part of her painful past, and instead of continuing law school, got her masters in social work.

Affirmations for a Healing Mother

- I attune to my healing ability to sustain and heal my creation.
- I use my healing energy to heal my Inner Child.
- I radiate healing energy to others.

Questions and Exercises to Discover Your Mother Archetype
Take a few moments to list of all the things you have given birth to: a delicious gourmet meal, a piece of art, a new business, a garden, a relationship, a child, a new place to live. Be aware of the creative Mother within you.

Imagine yourself pregnant with a new creation. It may be a child, an idea, a garden, a home, a business, a book, a piece of art, or a new awareness of who you are. What kind of physical, spiritual, mental, and emotional food are you feeding your creation?

Your creative energy dwells in your belly, your womb, your solar plexus, and your center. If you want to create something new—a baby, a book, a business, a fantastic meal, an addition to your house—take time to focus on your belly. Put your hands on your abdomen and imagine your power. What color is your power? Take some time to see and feel your creative power. Speak to this part of you and find out what this power wants. Feel this energy begin to move, and move your body with it. Begin to dance, to paint, to draw, or to write what is coming to you. Perhaps you see and feel nothing. If this happens, let your breath take you into your womb. Your creation center may need to be quickened with your breath. Breathe as if your air is entering and leaving your womb. Continue this practice through the day or week until you begin to feel your creative energy moving.

Think of something you want to create in your life. Do you feel frozen? What do you need from your Inner Mother to take the first step to thaw out and move toward creation? Sometimes this may require calling on your Inner Warrior to assist you in taking action. You may not know what you want. If this is the case, calling on the intuition of your Inner Crone to work with your Inner Mother will open the door to the garden where Mother Nature demonstrates the beauty of creation.

If you are feeling stuck, burned out, dead in some way, it may be time to get to know your Inner Mother energy and discover what she is cooking up inside you. The way to find her is to call to her: What do I really want to happen in my life? What are my dreams? What is my mission in life? What did I want to do as a little girl? What do I admire in other women that I wish I could do? If I could start all over, what would I do differently?

Are you smothering your creations? Have you forgotten who you are in order to please others in your life? Be aware of your breath when you are around others. If you find yourself barely breathing, you may be experiencing someone smothering you. The body wants to be free to breathe deeply and fully, yet in the presence of someone who needs to have power over you, fear enters and restricts your breathing.

Is there any part of your creation that fails to thrive because of your need to protect, to be powerful, or to be in control? This may be your husband, partner, lover, business, employee, client, home, child, plant, project, idea, or book. Take some time to consider all the things you create and decide whether you are smothering or providing nurturing, sustaining energy.

In what areas of your life are you withholding your positive Mother energy? Are your relationships flourishing or are they withering from the lack of your presence and attention? How is your career? Are you withholding your talents so others may shine? Are you afraid to put yourself out there, or is it easier to fade into the background?

Take a moment to recall what you were taught about relationships by your mother. Now recall a significant relationship in your life, including your relationship with yourself, and consider ways you are just like your mother.

Consider a time in your life when you have experienced critical energy. Was it from a teacher, a parent, a friend, a lover, a boss, an employee? What happens inside your body when you recall these times? What could this person have said or done to empower you to change? When was the last time you were critical of your creation as well as yourself?

Were you shamed by your mother? If so, what were the messages and how do these messages affect your behavior today?

To keep you from misusing your healing powers, ask yourself the following questions: What is my motive behind what I am doing? How is what I am doing serving my creation? The stronger your light and gifts of healing, the more potential you have of poisoning your creation.

How are you living your mission and making a difference in yourself, your family, your home, and your community?

Lynn Trotta's Story
Bracing myself against the bathroom mirror, I stared into my bloodshot and wet eyes and thought, "My life is over."

I looked again at the pregnancy test, admitted that the line was not faded but in fact a clear dark blue, looked back into mirror and thought, "Yes, definitely over."

It feels all very dramatic now, but at the time it was the scariest and truest thought I've ever had. I had not planned on having a baby, but I did know one thing: I had a choice in the matter. Just because I was an adult married woman didn't mean I had to have this baby. This realization of choice saved me in that moment. After the tears stopped and cognition returned, I sat down and made that choice. Yes I would have this baby, and I would do everything in my power to ensure that while this pregnancy was unplanned, it would not be unwanted.

I spent the next thirty-two weeks mourning the imminent death of "Lynn the childless woman" so that "Lynn the Mother" could be born. With the guidance of a great life coach, I sat down and listed all the things I would miss in my current life that would disappear once the baby arrived. Things like sleeping in late, endless hours in the garden, and spontaneous travel. I agonized over that list. I wept over that list. Then I looked at it realistically. Everything that I wrote down fell into two categories: I wouldn't really miss it or I could still do it.

No, maybe I couldn't sleep late every day, but I could arrange for my husband to take the child a few mornings a week. The same went for time in the garden, and I can honestly say that I've never spontaneously traveled in my life. In the end they were all just scary and untrue thoughts.

All of this made me wonder, "Were these thoughts what prevented me from wanting a child in the first place?" How often do we hold ourselves back because of unrealistic fears? And how often do our greatest gifts stem from the very thing we feared most?

In the end, I'm so grateful this is how my journey unfolded. Having the time to grieve my old life before the arrival of my daughter left me clear, grounded, and ready to receive her and our new perfect life together.

Chapter 8

Stand in Your Warrior

We gain strength, courage, and confidence by each
experience when we stop to look fear in the face.
We must do that which we think we cannot.
—Eleanor Roosevelt

Nothing is as strong as gentleness.
Nothing is as gentle as real strength.
—St. Frances de Sales

*As you walk through your sacred place, you meet a woman carrying a
sword and a shield. You stop and look at her in awe as you take in her
strength, her focus, and her fierceness. It is clear that she is on a mission.
She looks you in your eyes and says, "I am your Inner Warrior. I am here
to keep you focused on your mission and guide you to develop strategies
to get you where you want to go. I am here to teach you to stand in and
speak your truth. I am the one who protects you, keeps you safe, and
knows your boundaries. Are you ready to know me?"*

*W*arrior energy is often portrayed as fighting for one's country. However, there is another warrior: the Warrior within us that fights our internal battles and protects us from getting hurt. The Warrior archetype helps us to move forward, take action, and keep the vulnerable parts of us safe. She challenges us to find our strong, assertive, intentional, penetrating energy that protects and balances our tender feminine spirit.

Fairy tales have many examples of Warrior energy. According to Carl Jung, every character in a fairy tale, whether it is a man, woman, or even an animal, is a part of our psyche. Consider the tale of Rapunzel, who was locked in a tower by her wicked stepmother. Rapunzel is the innocent Child archetype who is controlled by her critical Mother archetype. She is locked up and invisible. Rapunzel stays alive by singing to stay in touch with her dreams and her joy. Her inner masculine, represented by the prince, or her Inner Warrior, hears her singing and frees her so she can become an adult woman and manifest her mission. Our Warrior inside us listens to our hearts sing and frees us from our imprisoned dreams.

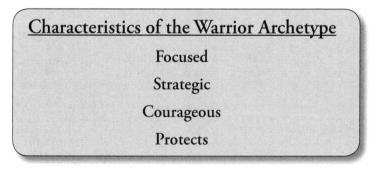

Characteristics of the Warrior Archetype

Focused

Strategic

Courageous

Protects

The Warrior Is Focused

Our Warrior knows what we need to do to stay focused on our mission. Every fiber in our body wants to protect and manifest our dreams. Our mission and purpose may change many times throughout our lifetime. For example, when I was a full-time mother, my focus and my mission were to raise my children and be involved with my family. In order to be with my family during the summer and vacations, I chose a career of teaching at a university.

As I continued teaching, my focus shifted to getting tenure, so I enrolled in a doctoral program while working full time. My mission and focus went more toward my teaching career and away from my family. When I became conscious of what was happening, I dropped out of my doctoral program, found a less demanding teaching job, and put my focus back on my primary mission: to be a mother and a wife.

If it is important for us to stay home with our children and be present for them, we can access our Warrior to find ways to manifest that mission. Consider the young mother who was an elementary school teacher. It became clear to her after a few months with her newborn that she did not want to go back to teaching, so she began researching how to start a day care business in her home. In just a few short months, she was providing income for her family and fulfilling her current mission of being a full-time mother.

We need our Warrior to help bring our mission into the world. If we just sit, think, mull, stare, and hope the inspiration will come, our Warrior is not activated. Our Warrior helps us take action so we can make a difference in the world.

Our Warrior knows we are unique and knows we have a right to live our mission and fulfill our dreams. We will encounter energies that want to take us off course, challenge our intents, and question our motives. Internal voices may tell us we have nothing to offer and say things like, "Who do you think you are?" In order to be seen and heard we need to access our Warrior who has the tools of strategizing, articulating, manipulating, and organizing to help us.

As women, we are hard-wired to do many things at once, so our focused Warrior helps us to accomplish our missions. We can ask for help, not only from our Inner Warrior but from others. Asking for help is a Warrior skill that can make a difference between a peaceful mind and a lost battle. When we accept the importance of our mission, our Warrior helps us maintain our priorities and stay focused.

The Warrior helps us figure out how to get what we want, whether it is money, a clean house, more time with friends, or a college education. The Warrior whispers in our ears, "You are on a mission. Keep going," especially when we want to quit. The Warrior takes charge of the present and keeps us on task, even when our to-do list and others demand our attention.

However, it is possible to focus so much on our mission that other parts of us get lost and forgotten. For example, some women are so focused on their careers that they neglect their families, friendships, and even their self-care. There are other women who are so focused on raising their children that they neglect their partners and friends. Their relationships with their partners may falter because they have lost touch with their Inner Lovers and are consumed by their Inner Mother archetypes.

An example of how we can focus too much on one thing is provided by my friend Mary, who is dedicated to raising funds for breast cancer research. Every time I call her, all she talks about is fund-raising. She never asks me about my life except to ask if I have donated money to her organization. Her Warrior energy to fulfill her mission drove me away, not only from her, but also from her cause. The missionary zeal of an over-focused Warrior can overwhelm and drive others away from instead of toward the goal.

Another sad effect of being too focused happens when a woman is so consumed with her mission that she loses touch with her sense of self and *becomes* her mission instead of *serving* her mission. This can manifest in chronic exhaustion and lifelessness.

Catherine, a tall, slender, thirty-four-year-old woman, was overwhelmed with her career and her family responsibilities. She wanted to be a perfect mother, a perfect wife, a perfect housekeeper *and* have a gorgeous body. As she looked at her life, she realized that she was destroying herself because she was focused on so many things outside of herself that she wasn't doing justice to any of them. Inside, she was depressed and lacked self-confidence. She hid her feelings and worked hard so others wouldn't know how she felt inside. Her body, her home, and all her external characteristics showed perfection, but inside, she was in shambles.

At a Woman Within Training, Catherine drew a picture of multiple arrows attacking her head and a black collar drawn around her neck to symbolize that she felt like a slave to her life. As Catherine explored these arrows and this collar around her neck, she realized she was working way too hard get the acceptance of her mother and her husband. Her focus was on others and very little on herself. She realized it was time to bring her life into balance by creating the life she wanted to live, not the life her mother or husband wanted her to live. Catherine let her house go a little, asked her husband to help more with the children, and told her husband and her mother how her desire to please them all the time was not serving her. As she followed through with this new focus, she felt more at peace, started a part-time job she had longed for, and had greater intimacy with her husband. Her Inner Warrior helped her to find her voice and use it effectively to achieve and focus on her new goals.

If there is too little focus on what we want, our Warrior becomes inaccessible. When we know our mission and have a sense of purpose, we filter everything through this lens and make clear choices. If we do not know our mission and our sense of purpose, we are easily swayed by everyone else's whims and needs and begin to lose the core of who we are. For example, let's say that a woman knows without a doubt that she has a talent as a child care worker. When she takes care of children, she feels more alive, more passionate than any other time in her life. Yet she doesn't take time to nurture this purpose; instead she listens to what other people tell her she should be doing, especially her dad, who tells her that she can never make a decent salary doing this kind of work. Another message may be "What do you want to do that for? That's a waste of time." She gives herself over to the spoken and imagined demands of others, does what her dad wants her to do, and ends up feeling sad and unfulfilled. She yearns to stay true to her inner calling.

Some women project their Warrior energy onto someone else and give up fighting for what they want. When I met Ellen, I was struck by her bubbly nature and her smile. On the outside she radiated confidence and a strong sense of self; however, inside she felt depleted and alone since her mother died. Every day she experienced waves of grief and realized that her sense of purpose died with her mother. Her mother was her cheerleader, her motivator, her guide, and her Warrior. Without her mother's physical presence, Ellen was paralyzed and unable to move forward in her life. When Ellen realized her mother's gifts were all inside of her and all she had to do was reclaim them, her sense of purpose and her Warrior were restored.

Karen is a twenty-six-year-old who used school, achievements, food, and isolation to hide. She felt angry a lot of the time and judged others harshly. She had lost her purpose in life and felt lost. She was able to focus on school and completed her master's degree;

however, she could not find a job in her field of study. At a Woman Within Training, Karen learned how to access her Warrior archetype so she could come out of hiding. She learned how to express her anger in healthy ways. She also learned how to use a permeable shield when others communicated with her so she didn't take on their judgments or criticism. This shield let in the love of others and kept out the negative things that did not serve her. When Karen learned to call on her Warrior, she felt like a free seagull drifting in the wind. She can now focus on connecting with others and let others support her.

If we do not focus our Warrior energy, we may dabble in many projects and find completion difficult. For some women it is more difficult to compartmentalize and focus because our brains can switch from the rational left brain to the creative right brain. In order to be productive and generate reports, books, and other tangible evidence of our skills, we need our Warrior to help us create an environment of focus and intention. It is a gift to be able to multitask and juggle details, and we need Warrior energy to decide which tasks hamper us and which ones serve us.

Affirmations for a Focused Warrior

- I am clear and focused on my mission.
- I am making a difference in the world with all I do.
- I am unique and have a right to do what I love.
- I know my limits and I can ask for help.

The Warrior Is Strategic

The key to developing Warrior energy is to honor our intellect and our verbal skills as we develop strategies for action. Our Warrior is resourceful. We can ask for what we need in order to get where we want to go. By surrounding ourselves with encouraging people who believe in us, we can accomplish each task.

The Greek warrior goddess, Athena, is depicted with a spear in one hand and a bowl or spindle in the other. The spear represents her strategic planning abilities and the bowl her creativity. Athena's animal totem is an owl, a symbol of wisdom. Like Athena, when we engage our Warrior, we use our rational thinking and intellect combined with our creative instincts and inner wisdom.

Our Warrior wears armor and carries a sword and shield. The armor and shield are defenses to protect us in the midst of verbal battles or challenges. Our sword is there to set and maintain our boundaries.

The shield keeps our hearts protected from attacks. When we use our shield, our Warrior stays present and listens to what others have to say without attacking back. We can deliver a clear message and own the consequences of our actions. To use Warrior energy is to know the depth and breadth of our inner strength and courage and to know we are in service to our higher calling. The stronger our values, the clearer our intent, and the deeper our passion, the more our Warrior is needed to defend and protect us.

A part of us may fear being hurt if we speak what we know is true for us. Many of us fear conflict and need to remember that not speaking our truth causes death of our spirit. It is vital for us to speak up be heard. If we withhold our truth or blast out our truth without using our strategic Warrior, we lose our grounding.

How we speak our truth is vital to our success. First, we need to get clear facts by asking questions. Then we need to assemble the facts in a logical, understandable way without letting our feelings get in the way. Our Warrior thinks and speaks clearly when we ask our Inner Lover to contain our feelings so we can communicate the facts. By combining our Warrior and Lover energies, we communicate with compassion, especially in a conflict. Think of communication using the following spectrum:

←――――――――――――――――――――――――――――――→

Brutal Honesty   **Compassion**
Truth with Compassion

The Warrior knows how to speak truth with compassion. If we are brutally honest, we do not care how the other person might receive our information. If we are speaking only with compassion for the other person, we don't care enough about ourselves to speak our truth, because we are afraid of hurting the other. We can speak our truth with compassion by using care and strategy to say what we need to say in order to serve the good of all.

In his book, *Warriors of the Heart,* Danaan Parry says, "It is important for the Warrior to be fully present ... in the midst of conflict." Our emotions may be surging, and we may want to run away from the situation or we may want to use our arsenal of words, our tongue, to cut our enemy to shreds. Neither approach resolves a conflict. Being in our strategic Warrior requires us to be present to ourselves and the other by listening with our body and mind.

It takes courage and resilience to stand in the face of fury and let the storm of another's wrath wrap around us. This does not mean we put up with abuse; it means seeing beyond the energy coming at us and recognizing that beneath this façade is a hurting, aching person. Transforming this energy requires the skill of reflecting back what was said to us. It takes great Warrior strength to communicate in a grounded, clear manner without letting arrows in.

Summoning our Warrior can be done internally without saying anything. During an exceptionally rough time in my marriage we went on a family vacation to New York City. On our way, my husband criticized every comment I made. I couldn't do or say anything right. At first, I took in all his judgments and criticisms and swallowed them as truth. I had an upset stomach from swallowing his criticism and I could not eat. This went on for two days.

Then my Inner Warrior told me to stop allowing these arrows in and to put up my shield. I imagined each critical remark as an arrow; I caught the arrow, took a moment to hold it, and silently asked, "Is this true about me?" If I found a grain of truth in his comment, then I owned it and worked on changing it. If there was no truth in it, I silently thought, "That is not true about me." I then imagined breaking the arrow and putting it down. In the past, I would have either shot an arrow back or swallowed it and acted like a wounded little girl. I did not tell my husband what I was doing; I just let my Inner Warrior take charge. In response to changing the way I reacted to my husband's criticism, he shot arrows faster and faster to get a reaction.

On the third morning of our trip my husband woke up and told me he had a dream that I vomited all over him, and he couldn't wash it off. From that moment on, his criticism ceased, my stomach stopped hurting, and our relationship took a whole new direction.

What happened? I stopped believing his projections (the vomit). I was able to own what was mine and discarded what was not true about me. Because I used my shield, his criticism of me did not pierce me. When I didn't let his projections in, he then owned and worked with them. My Warrior was protecting me from harming myself. This allowed me to use the information coming at me to fortify me, not destroy me. By being fully present in the conflict, I was able to know the joy of a renewed, more intimate relationship.

We can also use this strategic Warrior energy to help us in difficult situations. Lisa Hines, a Woman Within graduate, shares how she used her Warrior energy to help her son:

A few years after I was married, I had Jack, who would be the first of four sons. It was in his toddler years that my Warrior archetype emerged after a diagnosis of autism. I saw my bubbly, engaged, and vibrant boy turn into a drooling, slack-jawed, hand-flapped withdrawn boy shortly after an aggressive round of vaccines. I sat at the computer researching. Autism was scarcely heard of back then. I drove him to occupational therapy three days a week while he kicked and screamed at me from the back seat. By then I also had four-year-old twins who witnessed fifteen or so raging tantrums a day.

I blamed and shamed myself inside. Was I a cold mother, as the research indicated? Had I returned to work too early? Was a year of breastfeeding not enough? Every moment I could steal away was spent researching autism spectrum disorders. Every healing modality was explored—ABA, neurofeedback, wheat-free, gluten-free diets, massage, acupuncture, occupational therapy, speech therapy, vitamins, and so on. My instincts were in full throttle, and by this time, I was certain that vaccines played a role in my son's diagnosis. We had his blood and hair tested for heavy metals and found high levels of lead, mercury, copper, and even uranium!

By this time, Jack could barely speak. He stuttered and stammered and could not form words. This was the same son who spoke his first word at nine months! The more I researched, the more I applied to him and learned. Two exhausting years followed while we chelated his system by rubbing a sulfur-smelling substance on his back while he yelled and screamed, sensitive to the smell and wetness.

At the pace of honey spilling from a jar, my son was slowly returning. Sometimes he would make eye contact. Sometimes an entire sentence would emerge. I found later a correlation between copper and stuttering that no doctor had ever mentioned. Doctors and psychologists had no answers. It has been a path not for the faint of heart. I have raged when he was raging and felt guilty for it, but in every cell of my body I was determined to get him well. Now he is a few months shy of his fifteenth birthday with a full circle of friends, thriving in academics, and according to him, MIT bound.

If our Warrior becomes too strategic we tend to overanalyze and talk too much. Sarah is a corporate executive who has learned to use her Warrior energy to be successful in her career, but in every meeting, she talks nonstop and doesn't consider what others might need or want. For example, in meetings to discuss options for a business decision, when someone offered an idea, Sarah would object and give many reasons why this idea would not work and continued to push for her idea. Although all of her ideas were good, it was clear that she wasn't listening to anyone's input. The result was that the team felt disempowered.

Sarah has an inflated sense of self-importance and is preoccupied with her own ideas. Not only does too much strategic Warrior become the "all-powerful person" who thinks she knows what's best for her and for everyone else, she is volatile and reacts to criticism with feelings of rage. She tends to exaggerate her achievements and talents and needs constant attention and admiration to feed her need for power, similar to the tyrannical queen. Intimidating Warrior behaviors, such as criticizing, questioning, or demanding proof, destroys relationships.

If we do not allow our Warrior space to be strategic and instead let our emotions rule our decisions and communication, we feel disempowered and unable to take action. This happens when we are threatened and forget about our inner resources. Our survival instinct takes over, causing us to shut down, run away, or attack. We forget that we have a rational part of us that can think of solutions and filter out the intense emotional reactions. We may freeze and be unable to think and communicate.

Weak Warriors typically use a tit-for-tat method of fighting. This looks like, "You did this to me, so I will do the same to you. You didn't call me, so I won't call you." This may bring instant gratification; however, it doesn't empower our Inner Warrior or the relationship.

When we don't access our Warrior's strategic thinking or communicating skills, we let others walk over us as we try hard to placate them. We tend to operate from the too compassionate end of the communication spectrum, and we lose ourselves.

When we forget about our strategic Warrior, we may gossip about others in order to feel more powerful. Instead of inviting others to help us solve the conflict, we ask them to side with us and listen to our grumbling. In this situation we are caught in a rescue triangle in which no one can win. The one we are gossiping *to* becomes the rescuer of our internal victim, and the one we are gossiping *about* is the victim and we are the persecutor. Only the Warrior's balanced energy of strategic communication provides a way out of this relationship tornado.

Peg is a sixty-three-year-old woman who struggled with standing up for herself and learning how to tolerate people who hold opinions different than hers. When anyone disagreed with her, she just walked away. What she wanted to do as a career, interesting enough, was facilitate groups of people with diverse opinions to improve communication and understanding. At a Woman Within Training, Peg discovered what is blocking her from relating to others. Her mother didn't want a little girl and told her this again and again throughout her life. So Peg hid her feminine self by dressing like a boy, playing football, and acting like a boy. This false self drained all her energy to the point where she didn't want to exist. When Peg was able to embrace the feminine aspects of herself and risk taking off her boy mask, she began to feel vulnerable. She then imagined a fierce feminine Warrior coming to protect her fragile feminine self. She was able to balance both her feminine and masculine aspects. The energy of the Warrior also helped her to state her opinions, while the energy of her Lover helped her to stay and listen to others without running away. Peg became a successful mediator of groups after she was able to balance her inner archetypal energies.

Avoiding conflict is an indication that we are not using our strategic Warrior to serve us. We may think we have won the battle by being passive, but the battle continues. We are unable to make decisions or to speak out with conviction. We may become paranoid and cut off all communications in order to protect ourselves. In doing this, we also cut off the ability to grow and to live our mission. We need to respect ourselves and show up in our fullness in the face of conflict.

Affirmations for a Strategic Warrior

- I use my intellect to manifest my mission.
- I am resourceful.
- I speak my truth with compassion.
- I am fully present in conflicts.

The Warrior Is Courageous
Courage is the mental and moral strength to venture out, persevere,

and withstand danger, fear, or difficulty. The Warrior can stay present in the face of opposition or threats with firm determination to achieve what she sets out to accomplish.

The Warrior uses fear to fuel her courage. Fear is a strong emotion that we need to harness and use for our benefit rather than letting it stop us. When we face our fear, its power lessens.

There are two kinds of fear: real and perceived. Part of our brain gets activated when there is truly a dangerous situation that requires the body to either fight or flee. This survival part of the brain protected us as children and, in many cases, kept us alive.

This same part of the brain reacts to perceived threats even if the threat is not real, and our body's nervous system responds as if it is real. The Warrior within decides whether the situation is dangerous or is merely a perceived threat. As children we responded to threats in a way we needed in order to survive. As adults, often we react as we did as children in situations that do not merit a child's response. This reaction comes from our reptile brain, which does not know the difference between the past and the present.

To understand the Warrior, it is important to understand the brain. The brain stem holds all of our survival mechanisms, including fear. When we feel intense fear, the thinking, strategizing part of the brain, our frontal cortex, shuts down. When this happens, the small, primitive part of our brain is activated to make decisions even though the possibility of taking appropriate action is limited. The amygdala is like a computer that pulls up a program when we sense the data, "Warning—you are going to get hurt!" In these situations, the Infant or Child archetype dominates our body, and the Warrior archetype goes into autopilot or disappears.

The key to managing this reaction is to listen to the Infant, Child, or Adolescent archetype so that these parts feel heard. Knowing which part of you is activated takes self-knowledge, and when the Child, Infant, or Adolescent feels heard, the frontal cortex can switch back on, and the courage of the Warrior can be activated. The biggest reason for this brain switch is to keep us safe; however, if we always live in fear, the survival hormones tend to wear out our body and our spirit.

For example, as a child I was not seen and acknowledged by my father, a Baptist minister who was over-focused on his mission and spent every moment of his day and night either in his office preparing sermons or out preaching. I developed a survival mechanism of withdrawing into myself so I would not be hurt by watching my father close his office door every day or leave the house to go out and help others. As an adult, sometimes my Inner Child gets afraid and feels abandoned when my husband goes into his home office and closes his door without telling me he needs some privacy. If I see this as a perceived threat to our relationship, I withdraw and go within where I can be safe, and I live with the fear that I will be abandoned forever. At times like these, I need to call on my Warrior to tell me this is not a real threat and I am no longer that little abandoned girl and my husband is not my father and he is not abandoning me.

This irrational fear of the Child living in the adult woman can be defined as **F**alse **E**xperience **A**ppearing **R**eal (FEAR). When we become aware of what is happening in our body we can do a reality check by asking questions. For example, I need to ask myself, "Has my husband abandoned me, or does he just want privacy to make a phone call? Am I really safer by withdrawing? What am I doing to contribute to my feelings of abandonment?"

When we face our fears head on and see them as companions we act from a very different place. We need to locate where the fear is in our bodies and then put a shape, color, size, and voice to it. Our fear then has a dimension we can speak to and use as an ally instead of an enemy. For example, my fear often appears in my throat, causing me to go silent. I see my fear as a white, alien-like creature that is behind me with his hands around my throat. As I speak to this white creature, he loosens his hands on my throat. He tells me that he just wants to protect me from getting hurt. I rename him "Courage," thank him for protecting me, and ask him to walk beside me instead of behind me, so he can tell me when to be silent and when to speak up. Together we make an awesome team, and my Warrior is proud of my companion.

Too much courage causes a woman to forge ahead without taking care of her body and her relationships. She punishes her body by working too hard, too much and holding way too much tension. She deals with her fear by projecting it onto others through intimidation and silence. She derives pleasure from getting into conflict and thrives on dramatic situations. In groups, whether this is a family or a work situation, she stirs up conflict to get a reaction. Through her drama she feels powerful and in control, which is how she keeps herself safe. She may become aggressive and bully others to get what she wants.

Our work is to bring our Inner Lover in balance with our Inner Warrior, so we can discover how to open our hearts and still feel our authentic power instead of our false power. This was the work of Ann, who had been sexually abused by her father. Ann's mother knew that she was being abused yet did nothing to stop it. Because Ann was not protected by her mother, Ann lost all trust in women and took on the appearance of being in control of her life and her emotions. By getting in touch with her abuse and feeling the fear and confusion of being loved and violated at the same time, she was able to forgive her father and renew connection with him. It was harder for her to forgive her mother for not protecting her and keeping her safe from her father. As Ann's trust in women grew, she was able to balance her Warrior and Lover energy. She no longer felt compelled to put on a front of being ultra-competent or in control.

Julia's mother abused her physically and emotionally throughout her childhood. Julia stored all of these experiences in her brain stem and was petrified whenever she was in a group of women. She felt that she was a disappointment to her parents because she preferred to climb trees instead of dance. She refused to wear dresses and she spent hours in her room reading science fiction novels. Julia described herself as empty inside. She wanted to feel good enough and loveable. Her block to getting what she wanted was too much fear, which she felt in her solar plexus: the place of power in the body.

At a Woman Within Training, Julia was able to shift her messages of "I am alone. Nobody loves me. I am ugly. I should have been a boy." She felt these heavy, dark messages were like wearing a heavy helmet. She imagined her Inner Warrior removing her helmet to let rays of light shine on her head. With the light, Julia was able to create new messages: "I am supported. I am beautiful. I am glad I am a girl." As she lets these messages in, she embraces her Inner Warrior who fills her with strength and purpose. Julia commits to see herself as strong and to reinforce herself with these new positive messages.

Another participant at a Woman Within Training shared her story of how she did not have the courage to move forward. When Diane was six years old she witnessed an older child slump, fall down, and die in front of her. Since this experience, when she witnessed anyone get sick or faint she felt like she was going to die. She felt constant anxiety and told herself, "Something is wrong with me. You are going to faint and lose control. You are going to have a heart attack and die." These messages became her enemy, so

Diane had to summon her Warrior to face these false messages that have kept her from being courageous.

She visualized her Inner Warrior who came in and told her that she is smarter than these messages and that what happened to the little girl she witnessed dying was traumatic, however, now as an adult woman she has the tools to deal with what happens around her. When Diane brought in her Warrior strength, she felt she had won the battle, and her anxiety faded away.

Affirmations for a Courageous Warrior

- I am determined to accomplish what I set out to do.
- I use my fear as my companion.
- I am authentic and vulnerable.

The Warrior Protects

The protector emerges if our creations are threatened; she becomes the "bitch" who is needed to keep them safe. A bitch is a woman who knows how to protect her Inner Child and anything that is important to her. Just as a female dog protects her puppies, our bitch energy is our Warrior energy that protects us and our mission, which is vital to our survival and growth.

When I was ten years old I was sexually molested by a Baptist minister. As he fondled me he said, "Don't tell anyone about this." As a young girl, I was terrified and knew what he was doing was not right, yet I didn't have the skills to protect myself. As soon as I got home, I ran to my mother and told her what happened to me. She believed me and told me this would never happen again. The very next day she went to this minister and told him to never touch me again. This act of protection from my mother left me knowing I was worth being protected and lessened the impact of my abuse. She became my Warrior and modeled for me how to use Warrior energy.

There is an art to taking action and maintaining boundaries in a balanced way. For example, when someone confronts us, the balanced Warrior does not resist by pushing back or defending herself. She stays without fighting or fleeing. When we stay and listen, we make a strong statement of power and connection. We communicate our strength through our presence.

Our Warrior is responsible for helping us set and maintain our boundaries. Most women have had their boundaries violated in some way. These violations can be to our physical space, psychological space, or spiritual space. To hold and know our boundaries requires that we awaken the Warrior within us. We gather data from our bodies, our minds, and our feelings about what is happening around us and we use this data to protect our space.

One of the key characteristics of the Warrior is her ability to connect and be compassionate while keeping her boundaries strong. We can use our Warrior energy to support another person in pain, whether our child, partner, or friend, without needing to stop the other's pain or take it on ourselves.

When we listen beneath the words of others, we can hear their unspoken hopes and fears. This skill can be learned, even if the person is talking about the weather or politics. Beneath the words are a lot of codes to unlock how to respond to another person.

The Warrior always carries her sword, ready for battle, yet she rarely uses it because she knows and states her boundaries and is true to her own code of ethics. Our sword is an instrument of discrimination to cut off toxic situations. By being true to our ethics, we will know when and how to end something and move on. The way we use our sword to end a destructive relationship or a job that isn't serving us is to state our boundary and to hold to that boundary. When we are clear about our boundaries and ethics, we are rarely violated, and we rarely violate others. If we expect others to guess what our boundaries are, they will probably be violated. It's our job to use our Warrior to communicate our boundaries clearly.

Many women who have been deeply hurt by others build up a strong protective defense system and overprotect themselves so others cannot get close to them, and they need to attack others to feel safe. Their armor has become thick in order to protect their vulnerable Lover.

I have facilitated workshops for hundreds of men on resolving their mother issues. One of the most inherent fears of men is the power of the feminine to wound them. Because many women do not have their healthy, balanced Warrior awakened, they do not realize how deep their words can shame and wound. Women fight with words, which can pack the force of a piercing sword. When women recognize how the power of their words affects others, they can then balance their terror of being hurt with the awareness of how their words may wound others.

If we are so strongly defended and protected by our armor and our walls we keep everyone out and end up hurting and isolating ourselves. Barbara is a recently divorced woman who holds on to her anger and hurt against her ex-husband. She has full custody of their three beautiful children. Her ex-husband was so emasculated and disempowered by her sharp words that he totally disappeared. After a few months, he asked Barbara to see his children. She was so defensive, angry, and hurt that she refused his request. Barbara did not know how to protect herself in a healthy way. Her toxic behavior drove her ex-husband away from his children, hurt her children, and did nothing to repair her relationship with her ex-husband.

It is very scary to let down the walls that protect us. We think they will keep us safe. As a child, we needed these walls to protect us. As adult women, we have the ability to be strategic and take risks to reach out beyond our walls and still use our sword and shield to state our boundaries and protect ourselves.

If we are wishy-washy in our values or our boundaries, we will be easily swayed and be vulnerable to being hurt. We give in and value what others want and forget that we have not honored our boundaries.

In the early stages of developing the Woman Within Trainings, I did not know about my Warrior archetype. After three years of successful weekends, I knew it was time to train other leaders. Since I didn't trust myself and was not aware of my Inner Warrior, I designed a leadership training program led by a group of women whom I thought knew more than I did. I was operating out of too much Lover energy, and I thought if I loved and connected with others, that was enough. I remained invisible throughout the whole training. As a result, the training was disjointed, ineffective, and lacked the aliveness and connection to the mission I wanted to manifest.

After this failed attempt, a friend challenged me to step into my "tiger" (Warrior) energy and take a stand and be visible as the teacher of this program and teach what I know best. She challenged me to protect my creation, to stand in my fierceness and power and be seen. This was contrary to what I thought was the right thing to do. My desire was to include everyone and make everyone happy. However, by doing that, I abandoned myself and the organization. My Lover energy consumed me, and my Warrior was asleep. I took the risk to be seen and do what I knew in my deepest core needed to be done. I stepped into my Warrior and created a magnificent five-day training program for Woman Within graduates who learn how to be leaders of women by learning to lead themselves.

Yvonne is a twenty-eight-year-old single woman who had

worked hard to get an education and a well-paying job. She was very successful; however, she had eight siblings and an unemployed dad who were constantly asking her for money. It was very difficult for Yvonne to say "No" to her siblings and even harder to say "No" to her dad. She gave all her hard-earned money away and had nothing left for herself.

She became aware of her lack of boundaries at a Woman Within Training and began saying "No" with a compassionate, strong voice. As she practiced saying "No" she realized that she could also say "Yes." She got very clear about the power of her sword. She became aware that the Warrior's sword has two edges, a yes edge and a no edge. When she wielded her sword and said "No" to one thing, she was then free to say "Yes" to something else. This freed up Yvonne to use her sword to filter her family's requests and protect herself at the same time.

Yvonne learned that the handle of her sword represents her mission to succeed as a businesswoman. Some days it takes both of her hands to hold on to her sword and to make clear decisions. At the top of her sword she imagines two extensions that represent truth and compassion. When Yvonne got this picture of her sword, her body filled up with white light. White is the color of a powerful Warrior. Joan of Arc always wore white, and it is thought that when we dress in white, others respect and acknowledge our presence.

Affirmations for a Protective Warrior

- I use my shield to protect myself from criticism and negativity.
- I hold my sword to establish and protect my boundaries.
- I am aware of the power of my words and use them discreetly.
- I protect my mission with passion.

Questions and Exercises to Discover Your Warrior Archetype
Take a moment to find your Inner Warrior. Is she sleeping? Is she working overtime? What is her role in your life?

Can you remember a time when you didn't speak up when you wanted to? Remember how that felt in your body. What does it feel like to not have a voice?

When was the last time you really wanted to do something, yet you were afraid to try because you might not succeed? Have you been afraid to put yourself out there because you don't have enough money, time, energy, or education to do what you think needs to be done?

Keep a journal of everything you do and assess your actions through the lens of your mission and purpose. How are your actions fulfilling your dreams?

Take a moment to look at all the things you're doing and/or not doing that you want to do. Pretend that each of these is a pawn on your chessboard of life. How can you move them in a focused way so you can have a feeling of peace?

Is there an area of your life in which you lack discipline? Do you put all of your energy into a couple of areas and neglect others?

Refuel your engines and to do a maintenance check on all parts of yourself. Are you in danger of burning out? The downfall of the Warrior is to always be busy and burn out.

Transform your thinking into action. Great ideas are part of the creation, and it takes a Warrior to take action to make a difference in the world. What are some ideas that are waiting to be put into action?

Live in the now and take time to savor each moment, each situation, and each thing you see, in order to choose either action or rest.

Marcia Stone's Story

When I attended the Woman Within Level 2 workshop, I learned a lot about the different archetypes, particularly the ones in which I was strong and those in which I was weak. My weakest archetype was that of the Warrior. I had always been someone who "ate the poison" of other's snide comments, criticisms, or sideways looks. My boundaries were soft. In fact, I didn't know what boundaries were, and I certainly didn't know how to set them. I remember hearing the presentation about the Warrior archetype and thinking, "I have no idea what that would feel like! I'm no warrior!"

As I have moved through the stages of self-acceptance and knowledge that has been my Woman Within journey, I picked up tools to help me access and use my Warrior to help me own my space, ask for what I need, set boundaries, and, at times, fight for what I need. Here are some exercises that have helped me access my Warrior.

- Get into the yoga pose called "Warrior." Sink down into your body and feel your strength and groundedness. Standing mountain pose is also a good position for getting into your Warrior archetype.

- Stand face to face with a friend and press your hands against each other at shoulder level. Stand in tripod position, with one foot forward and one foot back. Push firmly against each other using your body. Sense your own strength as you hold your ground.

- Get down on all fours and imagine you could pull up energy from the Earth into your body. Breathe deeply. Get in touch with the energy at your core—in your solar plexus. Slowly stand up and keep breathing, your feet firmly planted on the ground. Feel how strong and grounded you are in this position.

• Beat a drum and feel the vibrations of sound in your body. Sense how the drumbeat mimics your heartbeat. Beat the drum faster. Move your body with the drumbeat. Then stop beating the drum and come to a standing position. Feel the energy flowing through your body once you stop.

These are all physical activities that don't require any words. I find that for me, words can get in the way of accessing the strength at my core that is my Warrior. For you, it may be different. I know one woman who set up a "throwing wall" in her basement. When she needs to have her Warrior voice heard, she throws empty tin cans at the wall, opens up her throat, and yells whatever her Warrior needs to yell.

Once you have accessed the spark that is your Warrior self, you cannot lose it. Whatever works for you will be there for you again and again when you need to hold your ground. I know that as women in our Western culture, it has not always been okay to say what we need or hold our boundaries. I am very grateful that I have found safe ways to speak my truth and ask for what I need using my Warrior.

Chapter 9

Find Your Gold in the Shadow

In the shadow is the gold.
—Carl Jung

We long to see the seeds of our divinity blossom but we have
forgotten that every seed needs fertile ground in which to grow.
That dark, earthy, essential place within us is our shadow.
—Debbie Ford

*Your journey through your sacred place may have been full of surprises
and new awarenesses. You feel awake and alive to the many parts of
yourself. You may wonder, "What more can I learn on this journey?"
Your Inner Queen appears to you and tells you that it is time now to go
down into the dungeon of your sacred place where the Shadow archetype
dwells—in the dark, unseen. You look at her with surprise and fear as
you wonder what could possibly be in your dungeon. She leads you to
a huge iron door and hands you a key to unlock the potential of the
unknown parts of yourself, your shadow. With a trembling hand and a
determined heart you turn the key in the door and slowly descend down
the dark steps to enter the dungeon of your sacred place.*

*T*he Shadow archetype is made up of many aspects of all the archetypes we have journeyed with throughout this book. Because the Shadow is multidimensional and pervasive in all the archetypes, we examine this archetype differently from those in the other chapters. It is necessary to understand the importance of the Shadow in order to find the "gold" within us. The gold of the Shadow archetype holds our souls, which is a symbol of our Higher Self or the God, goddess within us. Carl Jung teaches that the way to become whole is to invite in the parts of ourselves that we have denied, rejected, or found unacceptable. When we do this, we find we can then brighten and lighten our lives, which are reflected by our gold within.

Characteristics of the Shadow Archetype

Hidden

Denied

Unacceptable

Unknown

Trapped Energy

The dungeon of our sacred place symbolizes the part of us that holds our Shadow archetype—all that we are ashamed of, don't want to know or accept about ourselves, the aspects of ourselves that we work very hard to keep hidden away from ourselves and others. As we have journeyed through our sacred place so far, we may have discovered that some of the archetypes feel more familiar to us than others. If there was an archetype that felt foreign or unknown to us, we possibly have put that one into our dungeon.

For example, growing up it was not okay for me to express or own my Warrior archetype. When I did express my Warrior energy, I was seen as stubborn, criticized, and punished. It took me forty years before I learned how to set healthy boundaries with clarity. I thought that being a Warrior meant that I was masculine, so aspects of this archetype became my Shadow. That is why men in black kept appearing in my dreams, as I shared in my story at the beginning of the book.

Some women have a very developed Warrior, often because they were physically and/or sexually abused as children. In order to survive they developed very tight boundaries and as a result put aspects of their Lover archetype in the dungeon.

To know ourselves fully and step into our wholeness, it is important to know about the parts of ourselves—the characteristics we find unacceptable or have neglected—that we have locked away in the dungeon of our sacred place. These Shadow parts of us can serve us when we shine light on them; however, they sabotage us if they are left in the darkness. When we own and embrace the parts of ourselves we do not like or have ignored, we claim our power and balance in life. Our Shadow archetype is our source of renewal. It is an essential part of our personality that is waiting to be seen and known.

Our goal is to integrate parts of us that we have cut off or denied and put in the dungeon, also called the *unconscious*. Mining for gold in the Shadow is an endless task, because there will always be Shadow parts to discover. Our unconscious is as deep as the ocean. If we don't own our Shadow, it will own us and cause us psychological and physical pain.

To go into the dungeon is similar to diving from a boat into the vast ocean. Each of us is the pilot of our own little boat that represents our ego and our persona—that part of ourselves that we show the world. The vast, dark ocean represents what we don't want to see or own about ourselves. To discover what is in the ocean, we need to dive in to find what we have put there and bring those parts up into our boat (into the light). If we take too much information into our boat all at once, we may sink our boat, so it is important to explore the unconscious slowly and deliberately. If we ignore our Shadow, our boat may be vulnerable to some shadowy creature jumping out of the depths and overtaking it.

If I do not own my Warrior's ability to set boundaries, I will be vulnerable to others taking advantage of me and violating my boundaries. It is like a pirate overtaking my boat when my boundaries are violated. I may be sailing along feeling good about myself and all of a sudden I feel overwhelmed with anger and resentment. I look around my boat and it is full of people I don't like and I don't want there. How did they get there? I ignored my need for boundaries and before I know it my boat is about to sink! The good news is there is a greater part of us, called the Higher Self—the Divine Part of us—that holds both the conscious and the unconscious and guides us in when to go diving and when to sail onward. Our inner voice knows who we are and will not deceive us.

What Is in the Dungeon

Those things we don't accept about ourselves become our map to the treasure of who we are. As psychologist Erich Neumann said, "Only by making friends with the shadow do you gain friendship of the self." Everything about us that we don't love will become hostile to us; what we cannot accept about ourselves, we cannot accept in others. Thus, all our relationships will be affected by how we view ourselves. We violate ourselves when we criticize ourselves and focus only on our flaws instead of our beauty.

Our Shadow archetype is what we put onto others to hold that we cannot hold ourselves. Because we do not want others to see or know us, we wear masks, also known as our ego, to conceal what is deep within us. We can't see our masks until we look in a mirror, remove our masks, and discover how distorted our face has become. One of Carl Jung's beliefs is that the Ego and the Shadow come from the same source and exactly balance each other. To discover and develop our light, we must also develop our Shadow; one cannot exist without the other.

Just as the dungeon is under the ground, our emotional pain is buried deep in our body. Spiritual teacher Eckhart Tolle calls this our "pain body," where we hold all our painful emotions. It takes a lot of energy to keep our pain hidden from others. Often we may say to others, "If you really knew me, you wouldn't love me." Until we deal with the cause of our pain, it consumes us, sabotages us, and we may act in ways that hurt ourselves and others. Often we numb our pain with a variety of addictions, trying to make it go away.

Everything that our parents did not like about us as a child has been put in the dungeon. Everything our peers told us that was unacceptable if we wanted to be liked is stored here. Every part of ourselves that we don't love goes into our dungeon, and if it is not attended to it becomes hostile. As Robert Johnson says in *Owning Your Own Shadow,* when we were born we were a perfect person born into an imperfect family whose job it was to make us imperfect, just like them. So, bit by bit, the treasure and wonder of who we were was taken off and buried in the dungeon of our sacred place, a place where we were forbidden to go and explore. Who would think that some of the most magnificent parts of us are hidden in the darkness of the dungeon?

Janine wants to be a happy person. She feels she has everything she could possibly want—a great relationship, a place to live, and a job, but she is never totally happy and realizes that she never does what she wants to do, which is to be an artist. She never sits down and paints; she feels something stops her from trying. When she looks into her dungeon, she sees her mother and remembers how her mother always favored her sister. Her sister could turn anything that happened (a broken vase or an argument) into Janine's fault, whether she was involved or not. Her parents always believed her sister. When Janine told her side of the story, she would cry, and her mother would send her to her room or make her play with her sister for the rest of the day. Janine just wanted to be hugged and accepted.

As she grew older, the fights with her sister got bigger and blown out of proportion. To protect herself Janine would stay in her room to get away from her family. It was the only place she felt safe. Her family then called her antisocial or would say, "Why are you so secretive?" and they would call her supersensitive. She felt so lonely, so unloved, so unlovable, ugly, bad, fat … so she kept to herself because she thought her family didn't love her.

Janine never remembers being hugged or seen as special to her mother. Her mother just shouted orders: "Don't do this or that." "Your hands are dirty, wipe your feet, set the table, come sit with us." Her sister was always perfect in her parents' eyes, no matter what she did. However, her sister constantly teased her, hit her, and make her do impossible things for her. Between the ages of six and eight, Janine was so miserable she considered suicide for the first time. She dreaded going home from school.

One day Janine made a little "house" in the basement by putting a blanket over a bar and sat there writing in her fluorescent crayons on twenty or so pieces of paper, "I hate myself." "I hate my mom." "I hate my life." Her sister came home with two friends, snuck up on her, and took the papers and read them out loud, laughing. Janine ran upstairs to her mom and cried and cried because she wanted to explain, but she couldn't talk and was once again punished.

When Janine went to high school she began to drink heavily, stayed out all night, and had a boyfriend that her parents didn't like. Her inability to communicate with her parents made her bitter and icy with them. As a result, Janine did not trust people, and it was hard for her to make friends because she was so afraid of being hurt. She felt uptight, scared and jealous of others, and she wanted to be able to meet and enjoy new people without feeling threatened. She wanted to love herself and see herself as okay; however, because of her past experiences she thought she was defective.

By telling her story at a Woman Within Training to group of women who listened and accepted her just as she was, Janine was able to visualize her parents and sister in her dungeon and tell them how much she was hurt by their actions. She symbolically took the chains off her parents and her sister and led them out of her dungeon into her beautiful garden. She was able to see that the gold from her past experiences was how strong she had become in learning to take care of herself. She took this gold from her past and placed it in her future and began picking up her paintbrush and letting her artist come alive.

Our personas are shaped by the shadows of our past, the parts of us that have caused us pain. What we judge or condemn in another is a disowned or rejected part of us. Because of painful situations we adopted beliefs that drive our behavior. Perhaps we have said, "The devil made me do it," which really means, "My unconscious belief made me act this way." These beliefs contain gold when we get conscious of how they drive us. By changing our beliefs, we can change our behavior.

We may have put our anger, our spontaneity, our sexuality, our enthusiasm, our masculine traits, and/or our feminine traits in the dungeon. If we despised our mother, we may have vowed never to be like her and put all those traits we did not like in the dungeon. If we were abused emotionally, sexually, or physically, and we believed we "caused" the abuse, we may have put our sensitivity, sexuality, and our ability to connect with others in our dungeon.

Our reactions to others create what is in our Shadow. Besides our parents, our siblings, teachers, clergy, and friends help us create our dungeon, because we try to be what others expect us to be and deny who we really are. Ultimately, we decide what to deny or accept about ourselves and others. Everyone we meet is a mirror that reflects back what we do not like or admire. All of our external environment and experiences are our mirrors reflecting back our dungeon.

In the dungeon are secrets we have kept from ourselves and others. There is a gap between who we think we are and who we want to be. Our Shadow is everything that annoys, horrifies, or disgusts us about others. Repressed emotions are like anesthesia; not only is the pain blocked by ignoring them, so is the pleasure.

In the dungeon are all the parts of us that we refuse to own and the parts we judge to be unacceptable. Here are undeveloped gifts and talents, lost parts of ourselves, and our unexpressed potential. They are hiding in the corners of our dungeon, waiting to be discovered. These parts do not go away. They cannot be destroyed. Everything needs an opposite—positive and negative; night and day; high and low. The Shadow is a healthy part of us; we created it and therefore we can change it. But first we need to find what we have stored there.

Much of what we put in the dungeon is full of life-renewing energy and contains many golden aspects. According to Carl Jung, the Shadow is 90 percent pure gold, and the Shadow doesn't lie.

When we repress our gold, we are afraid of the magnificence of who we really are. Our Shadow is our servant to aid us in fulfilling our potential.

Poet Robert Bly said that from birth to the age of twenty we decide what parts of ourselves to put in the bag (dungeon), and we spend the rest of our lives getting them out of the bag (dungeon).

How to Find Our Gold in the Dungeon
When we first enter our dungeon it is very dark, and we wonder how we could ever find any part of ourselves there. We can shine our inner light to reveal what is there. Our inner light is our goddess-like quality that reflects back our goodness.

When some women enter their dungeon, they see people who have hurt them chained to the wall or locked in cells. Others see fairy-tale creatures like witches and dragons and other mythical images. At times, we may see nothing at all and need to spend time to discover what we have put there. By observing others and becoming aware of how their behavior affects us emotionally, we can find out what is in our Shadow. Other people reflect parts of us we either despise or admire. We project our Shadows on them, and when we recognize that what we see in others is really part of who we are, we can then take back these projections and own them. Instead of blaming another for what he or she is doing, we take responsibility for acting the same way. Every quality we see in another exists within us. The old saying is, "If you spot it, you got it!" When we accept all these aspects, we can accept others, as well as ourselves, as whole individuals.

When we are emotionally affected by a situation or a person's behavior, we have discovered gold in our dungeon. When people do things that irritate or repel us; or when we envy and admire what others do, both are reflections of what we have buried in the dungeon. By claiming these behaviors as part of ourselves, we find our gold within, and we free the person we envy or despise.

Roxanne is a successful therapist who continues to work on reclaiming the gold from her dungeon. At a Woman Within Training she worked on an incident that happened to her when she was three years old. She lived with her family in a very old apartment in New York City and accidentally locked herself in the bathroom and couldn't get the door open. She was frightened and was banging on the door for help. Her brother had to take off the bars on the window and climb through the window to unlock the door for her. When she came out of the bathroom her father was waiting on the step opposite the door and beat her for causing so much trouble.

It made no sense to her to spank a three-year-old child for such a thing, and she never forgot this traumatic event. As she shared this experience, she felt transported back to that day and felt the feelings of that little girl—the terror and pain as her father spanked her with great intensity and yelled, "Don't you ever lock that bathroom door again," which Roxanne heard as, "You are a bad and horrible person for making a mistake and making others suffer." Roxanne finally understood why trying new things were always fraught with anxiety, and why she stopped herself from doing what she wanted to do with her life.

That night Roxanne had a dream about her dungeon. In the dream she had to drive a carpool and she looked out the window and saw her big white van parked out on the street. She got her keys, but instead of going outside, she went down to the basement. The basement was set up like a living room with couches and tables, and there was an electrical outlet in the middle of the wall. She thought that to start the car and drive she had to put the car key into the outlet, but when she did she got a bad shock. She did it again and the same thing happened. She then thought, "How am I going to drive the car when I keep getting a shock!" When she woke up, she realized that she has been "driving her life from the dungeon." She now knew that she needed to get out of the dungeon and go outside to the vehicle if she wants to get anywhere!

Often women project the ability to be strong and powerful onto others and fail to realize they are already strong and powerful. The unconscious cannot tell what is real and what is symbolic. Many women put their good qualities into the dungeon because they do not want the responsibility of developing and living up to their potential.

One way to understand how our Shadow archetype shows up is to ask others to give us feedback about how they see us: our strengths and weaknesses. Our Shadow is more obvious to others than to ourselves. If we could see it clearly then it wouldn't be in Shadow! If more than two people say the same thing to us, whether we believe it or not, it is most likely a truth about who we are. By exploring repetitive behaviors, such as overeating, smoking, and overspending, we can discover the power and pain of our shadow.

How we use or respond to humor is a way to discover what is in our dungeon. If we find ourselves laughing at a joke that everyone else finds disgusting, or if we don't laugh at something that is supposed to be funny, we can learn about our Shadow. Both responses may be manifestations of Shadow around the subject being joked about. The way to keep the Shadow in the dungeon is to laugh it off—or to lose our sense of humor entirely.

Similarly, slips of the tongue are excellent examples of what's in our Shadow. Sharon, a vice president of a large corporation, was in a personnel meeting discussing a difficult employee. After all shared what they felt about this employee's behavior, words shot out of Sharon's mouth, "She is too pretty!" Her words carried a lot of energy, and everyone looked shocked and surprised. Sharon realized immediately that this was her competitive self who did not feel attractive, and she was very jealous. Afterward Sharon told her personnel manager that she had just demonstrated a Shadow eruption, and she would take the responsibility to look at this remark and how it may be affecting how she related to this employee.

One of the places to mine our Shadows is in our dreams and fantasies. By recording and studying our dreams, we can realize what wants to come forward to be looked at and embraced. Keeping a dream journal and even going into dream analysis is an excellent way to mine our gold. What may seem like rotten garbage may really be compost—fertilizer for growing something new inside of us.

How to Transform What Is in the Dungeon
The first step is to acknowledge that a Shadow part of us exists. When we take time to listen to our bodies and slow down enough to examine our behavior, we can name the behavior or projection. After we name the Shadow, we can then talk to it by personifying it and listening to it. If there is someone in our dungeon whom we despise or admire, we can imagine them in front of us and let them teach us about this part of ourselves.

Transformation happens when we take back the projections we place on others and own these characteristics—both those we despise and admire. It will be necessary to do this hundreds of times with many, many characteristics. These parts of us contain information for us that will increase our energy when we accept them in a new way, a conscious way that can serve us.

Withdrawing projections requires looking within to see parts of ourselves that we put in the dungeon and examining what we are feeling underneath the projections. When we find the story behind the feeling that put this projection there in the first place, this Shadow part of us no longer holds us hostage. After we listen to the story inside our head, we can accept ourselves and let go of the story we once needed to keep us safe.

Whatever is in our dungeon grows in power and energy and may occasionally erupt and cause havoc in our sacred place. For some, havoc may feel like a dragon or a wicked witch invading all the rooms of our sacred place. In our life, this may look like depression or feeling like a spell has been cast on us. We need to face the dragon or the witch and learn from it instead of running away or letting it consume us. Just like the Wicked Witch in *The Wizard of Oz,* who tries to keep Dorothy and her friends from reaching the wizard in the castle, so do these Shadow parts try to keep us from the joy of our sacred place. By developing our courage, our mind, and our heart, we can overcome this shadowy character and find our answers in our dungeon.

Ann, a forty-two-year-old woman, visualized a witch chained in her dungeon. On the witch's left hand was a glove with razors. Her right hand held all the creative artistic energy she had denied in an effort to get ahead in the corporate world. All the messages from men in her life, her parents, and her teachers were loud and clear in her head: "It doesn't pay to be an artist." Yet, in her heart, her hands, and her body she knew being an artist was her true path. She quit her job, bought a studio, and still sat lifeless, unable to let her artist out of the dungeon. She was the victim of her own creative spirit. Through a process at a Woman Within Training, Ann was able to cut the chains from the witch, take the razor glove off her left hand,

and transform the razors into a beautiful sword, which she put in her right hand. By transforming the razors to a sword she was filled with creative energy. She then knew she could use this energy to set her boundaries and say "No" to anyone who would discourage her from being an artist. With her balanced energy, she embraced and danced with the witch, who was now her friend.

How to Integrate Our Gold
After reclaiming our projections, we can use art, music, and movement to integrate them into our bodies. When our ego is strengthened, so is the Shadow part of us strengthened in a way that can no longer be elusive and catch us off-guard. One way to integrate is through ritual, such as writing letters to those who have hurt us and then burning them. Other ways are through screaming in a safe place to release any pent-up anger that is trapped there. Sometimes watching destructive movies or reading destructive novels gives an outlet to that part of us that wants to destroy the painful parts of the past. By doing something out of our ordinary patterns, our energy can flow in a positive direction to serve us.

As we get conscious of our behaviors, we can more quickly discover what part of us is being denied and needs to be addressed. I have done this is by observing my behavior, and if I am doing something that is not typical of me, then I ask myself, "What Shadow aspect is rearing its head?" Recently a woman approached me and asked if I would train her to lead the workshops that I teach. I quickly said, "Yes," not exploring what I really wanted, so we proceeded to plan how I would train her. We set up appointments, and I would forget them, and I didn't return calls and waited days before answering her e-mails. This was so unlike how I do business. When I stopped and looked at my behavior, I realized that I did not want to train anyone else to teach this workshop. I was acting nice, yet underneath my niceness was a clear voice telling me that I was not ready to train someone else at this time. Again my Warrior who knows how to set boundaries had been banished temporarily to the dungeon. When I was able to be direct with this woman and tell her my boundaries, she totally accepted my decision, and for me, it was like a huge burden was lifted from my shoulders. If I had not become aware of and integrated this Shadow behavior, I would have sabotaged the relationship with this woman and possibly sabotaged the workshop we were going to lead.

If we do not integrate our Shadow aspects, we will be drawn to people who will have the Shadow characteristics we refuse to look at. These people are our teachers and are there to assist us in confronting what is true for us and learn from them. As we begin to love what we dislike in others, we integrate this aspect into ourselves. By finding the blessings in the negative events in our lives, we transform them. Loving and accepting what we envy and admire in others, we bring our gifts and talents into our consciousness. By doing so, we take on the responsibility of using our gifts and talents to make the world a better place. As Marianne Williamson says in her book, *A Return to Love,* "It is our light, not our darkness that frightens us most.... Your playing small does not serve the world.... We were born to make manifest the Glory of God that is within us."

What the Results Will Be
Exploring the dungeon will positively alter our lives. Our Shadow completes us. By unlocking our dungeon, we can find a part of our real self, our true nature that has been cut off for perhaps many, many years. We will have more compassion for others and more self-acceptance. By embracing the traits we despise and admire in ourselves and others, we are made whole.

Accepting our Shadow allows us to expand and get back trapped energy and free ourselves from the grip of others. By healing ourselves, we heal our relationships.

Affirmations for an Integrated Shadow

- I am whole.
- I embrace all parts of myself.
- I claim my magnificence.
- I celebrate the gold of who I am.

Questions and Exercises to Discover Your Shadow Archetype
What are some messages you got from your parents that you still believe about yourself and are buried in your dungeon?

Think of people who irritate you and identify the characteristics that bother you. Take some time to journal about these characteristics and then consider how you might have the same characteristic in your dungeon. How can you bring them out to the light?

Think of people whom you admire and envy and identify the characteristics that you wish you had. Take some time to journal about these characteristics and then consider how you might begin to own and claim back these parts of you.

Are there any people chained in your dungeon? If so, list them and take some time to discover how freeing them may help you get unstuck in your life.

Spend one hour each day being aware of how you project your negative and positive qualities onto others—people you are in relationship with, and even characters on television or in the movies. Commit to take back at least one of these projections and own the responsibility of how it is affecting your life by keeping it in the dungeon.

Lisa Hines' Story

One night in the black-and-white light of the TV screen, while my younger brother sat nearby, my sixteen-year-old brother slid his hands up my legs and fondled me. This continued until he left for college three years later. The Shadow was in full force from that point on. I had decided, right then and there, that no one could know this dark thing that occurred week after week. No one could know, ever. I made a vow that I would "trick the world," that I would handle this all on my own. I smiled more than usual. I laughed. I pretended that all was wonderful every day that I lived in that house. On Sundays, when my family of seven took communion in the large cathedral church in our community, I walked with reverence and pride up the aisle in my ribboned dresses and white patent leather shoes. I knew that one day I would leave this small town that I was silently drowning in. Now, in reflection as a forty-eight-year-old woman, I see clearly the gold in the dungeon. The abuse was my ticket out. The intense repulsion jogged my engine, and the desire to leave and move far away was summoned early on. This gave me the courage to widen my experience and find my true self away from my family.

Chapter 10
Be Still and Listen to Your Crone

A Crone is a woman who has moved past mid-life
and acknowledges her survivorship, embraces her age,
learns from the examined experience of her life, and
appreciates the wrinkles on her face. A Crone is a woman
comfortable with her spiritual self, intuition, and creative power.
—Susan Ann Stauffer

As a white candle in a holy place, so is the beauty of an aged face.
—Joseph Campbell

*As you emerge from the darkness of the dungeon you find yourself in a
beautiful garden full of rich, lush greenery, colorful flowers, and trees
loaded with ripe fruit. The sun's rays dance upon the grass and foliage
of your garden. This is the garden of your sacred place, where you can be
one with the Earth and commune with your Inner Crone.*

*This place holds the cycles of life. Death and rebirth surround you as
flowers blossom, wither, die, and fall to the earth as they scatter their
seeds to sprout again. Here, you can be still and listen to your inner*

voice, the intuitive voice of your Inner Crone. You can come here to pray or meditate and celebrate the depth of your wisdom and your connection to your Higher Power. The garden is where you can come to grieve and let go of pain that no longer serves you—the pain of aging, the pain of loss, the pain of regrets. Welcome to your garden, the place of your Inner Crone.

When we think of the word *crone* we may think of a withered old woman. Messages from family, friends, media, and society tell us to hold on to our youth and beauty at all costs and at a great cost. The psychological cost is so high that many women put their Crone to sleep in their unconscious. She comes out briefly at moments of death to remind us of our mortality. She peeks at us in the mirror as we put on our face cream and wonder if we can find another product to remove any vestige of her from our faces. We silence her whisperings of guidance and reminders we are entering into our final stage of life.

This image of the Crone is changing today as women are reshaping the meaning of getting old. Instead of seeing themselves as being old and useless, women are stepping into this stage with a sense of accomplishment and pride, signifying that when they reach this stage, they have stepped into a powerful phase of their life.

The Crone completes the cycle of creation. She represents the part of us that withers and dies, and she is the part that holds the fullness of her wisdom to create new places of growth and magic throughout the world. She can hold the pain and joy of each moment as she celebrates both endings and beginnings. She keeps the keys of life and death and knows how to let go of what no longer serves her. She looks at life through the lens of both/and instead of either/or perspective.

Characteristics of the Crone Archetype

Spiritual

Intuitive

Ages Gracefully

Wise

Accepts Death

The Crone Is Spiritual

The Crone invites us to go within and to plant the gold that we have taken from the dungeon in the garden of our lives. She is the gardener of our souls, and by working with her and learning with her we can grow richer, fuller lives. Being a gardener takes attention and reflection. This is the aspect of the Crone that asks us to realize the "God(dess) Within."

To cultivate our garden we need to find the tools that will work for us. For some it may be prayer. For others it might be meditation or just sitting quite with a cup of tea to start one's day. The important tool is to listen to our inner guidance in the silence of our garden. Reading inspirational books may be a tool for some to get in touch with the spiritual essence of the Crone. Whatever tools we chose to use in our garden, the importance is to find a daily spiritual practice that feels right for us.

One of the languages of the Crone is silence. Mystic and spiritual healer Joel Goldsmith says, "Only through silence when the senses are at rest can spiritual power come through." Listening into the silence brings our Crone into our consciousness, and in order to hear her still, small voice, we need to stop what we are doing, be still, and listen. Because she is connected to our Divine Source, she can answer our questions like, "What is the purpose of my life?"

and "What is the meaning of my suffering?"

The Crone archetype is our spiritual connection, and she is seen in myths and stories. She has been seen as a witch and a magician. We can access her good energy by recognizing her power. The Crone knows how to use her power in a way that can serve us and others. When we get in touch with her power we have a responsibility to use it to make the world a better place.

Our breath is the gateway to our Crone archetype. We can use the spiritual energy of the Crone by watching our breath when we are angry, upset, or full of emotion. As we experience the emotion, we can visualize the color of the emotion and breathe it out of our body. As we inhale, we can visualize a healing color to replace the color of the emotion. We can do this until we feel cleared of any emotional energy that may be keeping us stuck.

We can also see an image of our Crone within us and ask her to place her hands on our body and send us healing. If we want the healing for someone else, we can see an image of that person and picture our Inner Crone putting her hands on that person.

As important as the practice of prayer, yoga, meditation is, we also need to listen and apply the Crone's lessons to our lives. Sally has too much of the spiritual aspect of the Crone. She goes to church three times a week. She reads her Bible and prays for an hour every morning. As challenges come up during the day she turns them over to God. These are all beautiful parts of the Crone; however, Sally has not integrated the lessons of the Crone. She hides her pain and suffering in her constant focus on her spiritual practice. She is escaping and circumventing her problems. She is not setting goals and taking action to meet her goals. Prayer becomes a crutch instead of a tool. If we use religion to hide our pain instead of finding the root or cause of the pain and moving through it, we have not fully embraced the spiritual aspect of our Crone.

If we are out of touch with the spiritual aspect of the Crone and deny our connection to our Divine Source, we may feel empty. Instead of spending quiet time alone, we fill up the emptiness with getting busy or drowning out our Crone's voice with all the technology of e-mail, music, texting, talking, and television. Internet surfing has replaced inner surfing and fails to fill up the empty heart. There are countless ways to say we don't have time to be still and listen.

A woman who denies the spiritual aspect of the Crone may become bitter, cynical, and critical of all aspects of life. Because she does not have faith in the process of life, she doubts the flow and process of life. Instead she worries and frets over things she cannot change and has no control over. Instead of listening to our Inner Crone, we mull over our concerns, regurgitating what happened and attempting to resolve impossible situations.

Affirmations for a Spiritual Crone

- I use the language of silence.
- I accept and use the healing energy of my Crone.
- I listen to the voice of my Crone and apply her lessons.
- I breathe with consciousness.

The Crone Is Intuitive

Intuition is another language of our Crone. The Crone is the part of us who listens to the language of Nature. By listening to the wind, looking at the stars, watching birds fly, and counting the petals on a daisy, the Crone teaches us the simple lessons that nature gives us every day if we just take time to be still and listen.

I learned to listen to the language of my Crone when my son

was missing in Africa. In January 1994, our seventeen-year-old son called us from Portugal to tell us he was going to Morocco, then across northern Africa, up into Egypt, and on into Israel. He told us he would call us when he got out of Africa. Five months later, we still had not heard from him. We called the State Department in Washington, D.C., who told us he had cashed $1,000 of American Express traveler's checks, which was almost all the money he had. My heart froze because I was afraid that he was dead. However, Nature had a different message. I saw crows everywhere I went. For two weeks, every single crow I saw was flying from south to north. Their message was that my son was traveling from the south to the north on his way home. I dared not mention this to anyone for fear I would be thought crazy. I was stunned by the consistency and constancy of this message, and I was validated when two weeks later I got a call from him saying, "I am out of Africa and I am coming home." He told us he had been living in a cave in southern Morocco and had no access to phones. What a relief to hear his voice and to renew my trust in my Crone! The Crone listens and watches for what the creatures and creations have to say.

Native Americans respect and honor the Earth and all its creatures. All food is recognized as a gift from the Earth. Native Americans believe that trees, stones, grass, clouds, buds, and animals can talk. By sitting on a rock, hugging a tree, or lying on the Earth, we can learn how to communicate with our Crone. Women create life through their bodies, just like the Earth. By becoming one with the Earth, we can be conscious of our environment and heal the Earth.

I was totally in tune with the Earth when I was walking with my ten-year-old son on a beach in Door County, Wisconsin, and came upon a depression in the sand. Without speaking, we spontaneously began to collect feathers, flowers, rocks, shells, even some bones, and meticulously put them in the sand. We silently placed seven white feathers and twelve black feathers in a magical and powerful way. We did not talk about the meaning of the mandala we created in silence; however, we listened to Nature and worked with Nature to make a sacred creation.

The intuition of a Crone is different than the intuition of the Mother. The Mother is more attached. The Crone is detached. The Crone intuition is bigger, reaching to strangers, friends, and colleagues. The Mother intuition is more focused on her children and her family.

The Crone knows that resistance does not serve her, so she becomes like a river, flowing to the powerful sea. When she becomes like a river, the stones of life no longer hurt. She soothes the stones with her constant quiet flowing motion. She realizes that others may wish to beat the river with a hammer or stick a sword in it, but water cannot be hurt in that way. She continues to flow around the obstacles. Therein lays the strength of the Crone.

Believing that all things are going to work out when everything is falling apart requires the faith of the Crone. Sitting in the garden, the Crone watches as the plants die and regenerate season after season. She waits for us when we face the unknown, and she holds a lesson and solution for us.

There was a time when my Crone archetype reassured me that she was in charge of my life and I needed to just be still and listen. After we had lived in Milwaukee for twenty years, my husband was transferred to a city that both of us said we never wanted to live in. I had a business and counseling practice in Milwaukee, and I loved our home and our friends. My Inner Crone kept whispering to have faith and trust. The search for a new home seemed endless. By listening and waiting, we finally found a beautiful place to live nestled in two acres of woods on a small serene lake. This place was like sitting in the lap of the Goddess. My Crone knew what was best for us.

If the intuition of the Crone is too intense, we may hear voices inside our heads, and our imagination may run so rampant that we are unable to balance reality with the true voice of the Crone. When this happens, we need to balance reality with what we are hearing by calling on other aspects of ourselves to check out what is true. Also, it is a signal that we need to quiet our mind through meditation to distinguish what is our chatter and what is our true Crone voice.

Women who possess too much intuition may be afraid of their own inner voices. To counteract the power they become hermits and pull down all the shades, lock the doors, and don't answer the phone. They are unable to filter the stimulus of their external environment and go to an extreme of protecting themselves.

Confusion is a common feeling for the woman who is bombarded with intuitive messages. Because she can hear her inner voice and is unable to discern how to use this information, she questions herself. She is afraid to tell others what she hears because she fears being judged, thought weird, and seen as crazy. She uses confusion as a way to deflect anyone who may question her true knowing.

If we turn a deaf ear to our Crone's intuition, we become psychologically deaf and cannot hear her still, small voice. Sometimes it is difficult to discern among the millions of thoughts that race through our heads and siphon out the voice of our Crone. Our Crone's voice is like an internal guidance system, similar to the GPS systems we use in our cars. If we continue to deny our Crone's voice, we deny the powerful GPS system of our whole being.

Another manifestation of not honoring the intuition of the Crone is a woman who abhors nature and sees nature as an intrusion on her life. Her home is void of live plants or flowers, and she doesn't like to work in the garden for fear of getting dirty. She only sees the bird poop on her car and fails to listen to the message of the bird. In other words, she focuses on the negative side of life and fails to hear the language of nature.

Because the intuitive sense of our Inner Crone may be very strong, we may become resistant to listening to it because we don't like what we hear. Instead of trusting what we know, we start second-guessing ourselves and miss opportunities for growth and change.

Affirmations for an Intuitive Crone

- I listen to the language of Nature.
- I surrender to the flow of life.
- I listen to the voice of my Inner Crone.

The Crone Ages Gracefully

One of the hardest parts about getting older is looking in the mirror and seeing our wrinkles, lackluster skin, grey hairs, double chin, and sagging breasts. We compare our aging image to the image of ourselves at twenty years old and judge ourselves harshly.

Each line on our face tells a story. The smile lines, the frown lines, the worry lines, and the scrunched waves of loose skin hold years of wisdom and experience. How we walk with our Crone archetype throughout our life determines how our aged face will look. It's like being adolescents again as we watch our body age and change. We become clumsy and surprised at the way we look and feel.

In order to accept the beauty of our Crone, we need to change our beliefs about beauty. Positive aging is a state of mind that is a source of happiness. We can now be bold and outrageous without worrying so much about what people will think. When our body is changing, we are being renewed every day. When we look in the faces of older women, we can see past the wrinkles and see a glow that comes from their center and lights up their eyes and face. Marion Woodman, author of many books for women and one of my beloved teachers, is an example of this beauty. Her spirit radiates from every pore of her skin and love pours from her eyes.

As we saw in chapter 4 on the magical Child, we are in touch with this magical, spiritual energy at a very young age. Our magical energy never leaves. We leave it. We can call it back as we let the maturity of our years build on our childlike magic. Our child was able to play and be free without worrying what others thought about her. So it is with the Crone. At this stage a lot of the responsibilities of raising a family, advancing in a career have passed, and it is now time to once again play with abandonment.

Another aspect of aging gracefully is the ability to laugh at ourselves about the changes in our bodies and look at life through the eyes of experience so we can now laugh at our mistakes and the things that once got our shorts in a knot. Laughter heals us. When we can laugh so hard we wet our pants, we have released more than our bladder; we have released endorphins that can lift our spirits and help us to soar above the mundane parts of life.

When we accept our Crone we accept our aging. Often we are afraid of getting old and ugly. We experience the daily reminders of decay and degeneration ... fading eyesight, painful joints, a protruding abdomen, gray hair, a general feeling of tiredness. When we grieve the loss of our physical beauty, we can cultivate our inner beauty and focus on what keeps us vital and alive—exercise, healthy food, meditation. It is the fall of life, and it is time to go within and be with our Inner Crone instead of running away from her.

Another change our Crone can guide us through is the transition of retirement. This is a time of letting go of who we once were, grieving the loss of our youth, and taking steps to reinvent ourselves in a new way. This is a time to cultivate our inner sacred place and rest, similar to the cocoon in the Adolescent archetype.

The Crone knows that the best thing about getting older is the freedom that comes with being comfortable with who we are. It is time to do let ourselves be colorful and outrageous. We can wear purple with red, as Jenny Joseph's poem "When I Am an Old Woman" gives us permission to do. We don't have to put as much energy into worrying about how others will see us; however, we also don't go around disheveled. We are less attached to pleasing others. The more we explore and accept our gifts and limitations, the more individualistic and unique we become. We spent years trying to be like everybody else. It is now time to be who we are.

For many of us, our culture and our parents have taught us to be afraid of getting old and to avoid it at all costs. My mother was always ashamed of her age, and she would never tell anyone how old she was. When she was ninety-three years old, my sister got her a cane because she was unsteady on her feet. When she saw the cane she said, "I'm not using that. That is for old people!"

Some women fear aging so much they become invisible. Instead of trying to look good, they let themselves go and don't exercise, eat healthy, dress well, or use makeup. Other women attempt to dress like teenagers and go to great extremes to look young. We need the Crone archetype to help us balance our ability to accept our age without covering up our aging process.

Not letting go of the past creates a prison. Letting go allows us to step into the flow of life. We don't need to fix or change anything, only allow the fullness of who we are to blossom. As some women age, they become extremely afraid they are going to become bag ladies with no income, no friends, no home, no clothes, and nothing of value to do. If we focus on the fear of aging, we lose the beauty of living one day at a time.

Affirmations for a Crone Aging Gracefully

• I celebrate the beauty of my Crone face.

• I accept and embrace the changes in my body.

• I am colorful, outrageous, and laugh at myself.

The Crone Is Wise
The wisdom of the Crone comes from her ability to use her years of experience to deal with the problems that come up in her life. This deep archetypal wisdom is passed down to us from generations. She holds the keys to unlock the mysteries of our darkness, our past, and our womanhood. Our mothers and our grandmothers hold the wisdom of the Crone, and as we enter this stage of life, we pass on our wisdom to our daughters, granddaughters, and other men and women.

The wisdom of the Inner Crone is unique because of her ability to listen to someone else's pain without taking it on. When someone shares their pain with her, she imagines a ball has been placed in her hands to hold for a little while. As she holds the ball with reverence and knowing, she shares her wisdom and tosses the ball back, infused with her Crone wisdom. It is through this process that healing occurs.

This ability to hold our own pain separate from another's is called *containment*. When we are in alignment with our Inner Crone, we can be in chaotic situations and hold energy of strength and knowing. As we hold this energy, we stay detached from the situation instead of getting caught and twisted in it. This allows the whirlwind to find a level ground and swirl into a place of peace because of the presence of the Crone.

Another aspect of the Wise Crone is Grandmother energy. Something strange and magical happens to a lot of women when they celebrate their fiftieth birthdays. When I turned fifty, an urge to have a grandchild rose in my body, even though at the time my sons were not planning to have children.

Several years later we received a box of string cheese from our oldest son. Inside the box was a riddle that read, "A new bud blooms on the family tree." I jumped around and screamed with joy. My husband coined my antics as the "Grandmother Dance." At last, I was going to be a grandmother!

Then it happened again. My youngest son sent a package with two white decorated T-shirts, one for me and one for my husband. On the front of each shirt was a picture of water, islands, and mountains and on the back was a picture of a bumble bee. On the back of my shirt were the numbers 2/5/4. By the picture of water on my husband's shirt was the word BAY. I looked at the shirts trying to recall when we had visited these places together, and the bumble bee and the numbers made no sense at all. My husband came in and picked up his shirt, looked at the front and said, "BAY," then he looked at the back and said, "BEE." Immediately I heard it. *Baby!* I screamed and tears were running down my face in surprise, joy, and celebration. The numbers indicated the due date, which was February 5, 2004. I did my Grandmother Dance *again!* I am now the proud grandmother of four beautiful grandchildren.

Grandmother energy comes with age. No one told me this desire was going to rise up in me. Grandmother energy is very special and different than Mother energy because it is infused with the wisdom of the Crone. Even if a woman never has grandchildren, she still holds this energy for our Earth and all living things.

An example of how imagining that our grandmothers can heal our losses was experienced by Alicia at a Woman Within Training. Alicia had lost a baby due to an ectopic pregnancy when she was thirty years old and was afraid she could not have children. In order to grieve the loss of this baby, she closed her eyes, imagined holding the baby she lost, and thanked it for entering her body for a short time. As she sobbed and said good-bye, she imagined her grandmother coming to her and taking the baby from her. As Alicia handed her baby over to her grandmother, she felt a deep sense of peace in her belly and a huge burden lifted from her shoulders.

We need to take time to let ourselves be bathed in our own wisdom and the wisdom of our mothers and grandmothers. We discover our true essence as an ancient, wise gift as we get to know our Inner Crone.

If a woman tries to force her wisdom onto others, her efforts will probably backfire. Perhaps we have someone in our lives who is very wise, yet we hesitate to ask her for advice because when she shares her wisdom it comes out as shameful, and we leave feeling stupid or crazy for talking to her. When a woman gets stuck in wanting to always share her wisdom, she does not listen and is sometimes way off base in knowing what someone needs—which may be to just be still so she can hear her own Inner Crone wisdom.

When too much Crone wisdom overtakes us, we become frustrated if others won't listen to us and take in what we consider to be great wisdom gained from years of experience. Instead we become cranky, irritable women who are selfish and self-centered—a crotchety or cantankerous Crone.

When someone asks for advice, we are free to share our wisdom. If we give unsolicited advice, we need to examine whom we are really trying to impress. When we share our wisdom without another's permission, we violate their ability to search inside first.

If a woman says to herself, "I will never know anything worth sharing with others," she is denying her wise Crone. For many years, I denied the part of my Crone that told me my wisdom was worth sharing. When I was able to be still and listen, she poured her wisdom into this book.

When we doubt ourselves and our wisdom, we cheat others by not sharing our experience and what we have learned through the years, which is priceless. We never stop gaining wisdom. We learn the value of taking our past experiences into our present to enrich our future. When we take the time to let our Crone wisdom flow, we tap into an endless and rich resource.

Affirmations for a Wise Crone

- I am wise.
- I honor the wisdom of my heritage.
- I am grandmother of many.

The Crone Accepts Death

Death is a part of the cycle of life that the Crone understands and holds with reverence and grace. Sadly, many of us have not learned how to face and explore the meaning of death. Just as the garden holds death, so does every experience in our lives. Death requires us to grieve and let go of the past and move into the future so we can give birth to new opportunities. Without acknowledging and honoring death, we cannot step into the fullness of life.

Kerstin Bandura, a Woman Within graduate from Germany, shared, "My mother has cancer and the doctors said there is no hope for her. The Crone archetype is helping me to accept this diagnosis, to accept the finiteness of life. It is also helping me to accept her decision for the treatment that feels right for her—even if I have felt differently. And the Crone is helping me to be with her with gentleness and so much love."

Part of accepting the Crone is to honor her with a ceremony when we enter the Crone stage of life. For most women this is when they go through menopause. For me it was when I had my uterus removed. After many months of discomfort and increasingly heavy bleeding, I was advised at the age of forty-seven to have a hysterectomy. So I prepared for surgery by donating my own blood, arranging for child care, and asking my women's circle to be there for me through prayer and presence. Loss of my uterus was a marker for a transition in my life, so I asked my gynecologist to give my uterus back to me after the surgery. She was intrigued by such an unusual request and got the okay from the pathologist and other hospital administrators. I was discharged from the hospital with my flowers, get-well cards, and my uterus floating in formaldehyde. My uterus held the magic of my menstrual cycles and the creation of my two sons. It was a deep meaningful symbol of my womanhood that I did not take lightly. I wanted to let go of my uterus and move into my Crone in a ceremonial way.

On a cool, breezy October day in Wisconsin, my women's circle drove to a bluff overlooking the beautiful, blue waters of Lake Michigan. The sky was overcast as we gathered to initiate me into my Crone to mark the ending of my ability to give birth and the beginning of a new phase of my life. First we prepared the burial ground by digging a deep hole with our shovels and pickaxes. Then we built a fire in a hollowed-out part of the land and used the Native American practice of spreading cornmeal on the Earth and smudging each other with sage and cedar to create a sacred space.

We each gave thanks for this time together as women and drummed to connect ourselves to the Earth and to our hearts. We spoke about the meaning of our birth names. Pain and joy were mingled as we shared what it was like being born a girl. Next, we shared stories about our periods, how we learned about them, what they were like, and we released the shame that had shrouded this miracle of being a woman.

Our next round of sharing was about giving birth to our children. Tears of regret and joy flowed as we each shared what is was like being a mother. Some of us grieved our decisions to have abortions, and some of us shared what it was like not to have given birth to children.

We then honored the transition into menopause. One of the women honored me with a poem she had written. I then took on a new name, Dancing Owl Woman, and we went to the prepared burial ground. I placed my uterus in the ground, and each woman put in an object that represented something she wanted to release and transform. On top of these symbols of our past we planted a maple tree and flower bulbs to symbolize death and rebirth coming together to heal and make whole. We took the dirt in our hands and covered my uterus, the roots of the tree and the bulbs, knowing the magic of rebirth will come again. We sang a song and affirmed the power of our Inner Crones. In silence, we picked up our shovels and returned home with renewed faith in the cycles of life.

According to Carl Jung, the first fifty years of a woman's life are about learning how to live and the second fifty years are about learning how to die. The Crone archetype teaches us how to grieve, how to experience loss, how to let go. She is the keeper of the cycles. Like the goddess Hecate, she stands at our crossroads to guide us through our endings and beginnings.

The Crone archetype is with us throughout our lives and

prepares us for the final stage our lives. She reminds us that death is part of the cycle of life. As a child I was taught to avoid death, and if I experienced a loss I must not cry, because crying is a sign of weakness, not strength. Growing up in a minister's home, I attended many funerals, and the conversation afterward was about how strong the family members were who didn't cry. I never learned that it is necessary to cry and express the depths of my grief.

My eight-year-old son taught me how to grieve when we had to put our dog, Midnight, to sleep. Our dog had an advanced stage of heartworm disease, so we said good-bye to him and thanked him for all the gifts and joy he had brought us. We hugged his warm body and drove in silence to the vet. As the veterinarian injected him with a lethal dose of medicine, we watched as life faded from his brown, sad eyes. We lovingly wrapped him in a blanket and drove back home to bury him.

We dug a grave in our backyard and placed Midnight's stiff body deep in the ground. My son was crying and wailing from the depths of his being as he screamed out Midnight's name over and over. From the grave he took handfuls of dirt and put them on top of his own head. In that moment I witnessed the primal grief energy of the Crone. She goes down into the cauldron of the grave and becomes one with the Earth in order to experience death.

I was so touched by my son's expression of grief that when my father died, I wanted to experience the cauldron and grief of my Crone energy. It was important for me to take the Earth in my hand and to throw clumps of dirt into my father's grave to touch my grief and let go of this man who had a big part in shaping my life.

I talked to the funeral director of the small town in eastern Kentucky and told him my family and I wanted a moment at the grave before they covered the coffin with dirt. After the prayers and final words of the pastor, all the people left the gravesite, and the gravediggers came out from behind the trees. They removed the fake grass and lowered the casket into the ground. Before they bulldozed the pile of dirt, the funeral director signaled our family to come and look down at the casket in the deep hole in the Earth. Scooping the dirt into our hands, we threw it into the grave and heard the rocks and clumps of dirt thump on the metal casket that held my dad's body. Each handful represented anger, sadness, forgiveness, and acceptance. With each handful I released my grief. I felt my Crone come in to serve and heal me.

Every season of the Earth, the eating and digestion of food we eat, the morning and the evening of each day teaches us that life is a cycle. The night and the day are actually deaths and births. Going to sleep is a mini-death and waking up is a mini-birth. So the Crone is with us all the time. Welcome her.

If a woman gets stuck in always thinking about death, life becomes dark and dreary and her mind is filled with depressing thoughts. Instead of seeing death as a natural part of life, the thoughts become demons that lurk behind and around her.

If we get stuck in our grief and fail to grieve our losses in life as they happen, we carry a lot of baggage to the grave with us. We may carry resentments and unfinished business with loved ones, lost opportunities, relationships, and other losses. Failure to forgive those who have hurt us creates a bitter, withered crone.

Yet some women deny the existence of death. We don't want to talk about either our own death or that of those dear to us. We believe if we don't acknowledge it, it will go away. This denial shows up through hoarding material goods and hanging on to relationships that no longer serve us. The pain of learning how to detach becomes too great and the accumulation of "stuff" creates a false sense of security. Some women use drugs and alcohol to numb the feelings about the reality of death. Being unwilling to face loss robs us of joy. Staying with the pain heals the pain. When we let go we can live more fully. Our life is worth getting our heart broken many times if we walk through the pain.

If we deny the possibility of our death or the death of our partners or parents, we fail to plan, which puts the burden onto our family. It is important to think about how we want our last days of life handled, our finances distributed, and our life celebrated. This relieves our loved ones from burdensome details so they can be freed up to grieve our passing.

As painful as it is to sit down and talk about the final phase of life, our own or our loved ones', procrastination only intensifies the need to take care of the basics of the end of life. In the case of our parents, we can ask them to write a "love letter" that outlines all the vital information we need to know—where their finances and important documents are kept, and whom to call to take care of their material goods.

If we have adult children, it is our responsibility to write a "love letter" to them once a year with this information, so they can know what to do in the event of our death. If our children are young, we need to provide a will for someone to take care of them and our affairs in the event of our death. If women do not have children, then it is important to write a "love letter" to their partners or dear friends to let them know this information. For some women, it is a special nephew or niece that they feel connected to and trust.

Affirmations for a Crone Accepting Death

- I accept the reality of death.
- I embrace the Crone stage of my life.
- I grieve and let go of my losses.

Questions and Exercises to Discover Your Crone Archetype
Visualize the Crone within you. Let her body, face, and presence emerge. Imagine her standing before you. Touch her face. Feel her presence. Ask her a question and listen to what she has to say.

Close your eyes and visualize a garden. Take a moment to let your mind, body, and spirit create the sounds, sights, and sensations of a garden. Walk around your garden and breathe in the fragrances and touch the flowers and taste the nectar. When you are struggling with an issue, ask for a message from Nature. Be still and listen to Nature.

Take time to experience your feelings 100 percent. When you are sad, be sad. When you are angry, be 100 percent angry. Surrender to your Crone and let her carry you through to the other side of the emotion.

Be still and listen to her every day through meditation, yoga, prayer, or whatever spiritual practice works for you.

When you are feeling pain and tension, contain what is going on in the moment. If you are feeling hurt—deeply feel the hurt. If you are feeling joy—deeply feel the joy. Let the containment be like a chemical reaction in a test tube that can transform your hurt or joy. Containment is hard work, particularly when you want to explode or stop the pain with alcohol or drugs or any other kind of addiction. Containment may look like rest, however, it is really a transformational skill that a Crone can use to heal and grow.

Take a moment to consider a time in your life when you were resisting another person, making a decision, or looking for a new way of doing something. Imagine what it would be like to become like a river and just let your mind, your emotions, and your spirit flow with your thoughts. Instead of resisting, surrender to the power of flow. Go around the obstacles instead of using up all your energy to resist what is in your way. That is the way of the Crone.

To get in touch with your inner wisdom, take a moment to visualize your mother's face. See the depth of wisdom on her face that reflects the trials and triumphs of her life. Run your fingers across her face and feel her wrinkles. See the sadness and grief and joy in her brow. Look deep into her eyes. What wisdom is there? Listen as she speaks to you words of wisdom. Her words may be simple. They may be words you have heard a thousand times. Let yourself hear them differently this time. Hear the wisdom beneath her words. Hear the wisdom of her wise feminine soul. Do this same visualization with your grandmothers and aunts and even older sisters.

Create a Crone ceremony to celebrate your transition from middle age to Crone age. Invite in your Crone.

Grieve your losses as they happen to you. Do not grieve alone; share your sorrows and your pain with those who can hold your grief with you.

Be outrageous and let your colorful Crone have a wonderful time.

Judith Pauly's Story
In my eighth decade of life, it is exciting to be active and embodying the Crone archetype. She has allowed me to become all that I am as I embrace this latter phase of life. I like to describe myself as an outrageous, spiritual, creative, wacky woman with an inner intuition that borders on clairvoyance. Even as a young child, many of the Crone's qualities of wisdom and acute awareness were part of me. The ability to see beyond the obvious and be present with others was developed early on as necessary to have the "right to be." My early childhood was much about abandonment and loss. Never really belonging.

As the years rolled by, much of my identity connected with the eclectic and creative. The Yiddish term that could apply to me as a Crone is *meshugana*. Don't really care what others think and at the same time wanting to do the right thing. I am sometimes seen as "a rule breaker." I claim this is accurate only when the rule doesn't make sense. Rules and structure are part of integrity, and this is a positive characteristic of my Crone sometimes.

Open to all possibilities and relishing "signs or intuitive hits" is a very fun part of my personality. Finding several different ways to look at a situation is another fun game to play. I recently was visiting my daughter and grandson in New York City for the weekend. On Monday morning I had an appointment with a client in New Jersey. I was carrying a roller bag, a backpack with computer, and another slippery bag. I found myself at the very crowded rush-hour train. Imagine this seventy-six-year-old redhead, dragging and schlepping multiple bags, pushing her way into a subway train. The door tried to close, and I pushed my way in, only to step into an eight-inch gap between the platform and the train car. My leg went all the way down and I fell. New Yorkers can be kind. They helped me up, gave me a seat, and as I entered the train I said, "It is always my intention to grow old gracefully." Except for bruises and a momentary scare of the train pulling away and dragging me along, I am fine.

The outrageous part of the Crone was able to look back at this experience and laugh and declare, "I am really alive."

Chapter 11

Celebrate Your Wholeness
and Receive Your Blessings

I think wholeness comes from living your life consciously
during the day and then exploring your inner life
or unconscious at night.
—Margery Cuyler

Integration feeds our spirit and our soul as we ripen with wisdom
and compassion from our varied experiences. We mature into full,
integrated human beings with divine richness in our souls and spirits.
As we feel ourselves become whole, we can finally say
"How wonderful!"
—Wendy Palmer

As you leave the garden of your sacred place, you feel renewed, refreshed, and at the same time, ancient. Your journey through the rooms of your sacred place is almost complete. There is one last room to experience. The Great Hall is the last room of your experience. It is a place of celebration and feasting.

Your Inner Queen meets you at the door of the Great Hall. In the center is a large round table filled to overflowing with festive food. Music drifts through the air, and candles are lit around the room. She leads you to a beautiful throne where you will receive your gifts and blessings. She tells you that all parts of you are here to celebrate and bless your wholeness and magnificence. You take a deep breath and slowly take in the archetypal images of who you are. Your Woman Within is full of gratitude for this journey during which you have discovered and reclaimed hidden, ignored, or forgotten parts of you. Breathing in all these aspects fills you with pride and compassion for your past that has created the magnificent woman you are. It is now time for each of your archetypes to offer you a blessing.

You pick up your Infant self and look deep into her eyes and see your innocence reflected back to you. She blesses you with your ability to trust yourself and others. Her presence infuses you with the warmth of knowing you can always call on her when you doubt yourself—to recall your Divine spark. You gently place her into your Inner Mother's arms and feel the wholeness of knowing she is the perfect mother—your Inner Mother—to take care of her. You can stop blaming your birth mother, or the mother who raised you, for not being there for you in the way you needed.

You look in your Inner Mother's eyes as she holds your Infant self, and you thank her for taking on this responsibility. She looks back at you with the blessing of unconditional love. She gently puts your Infant self safely in her crib and takes you in her arms and blesses you with a nurturing embrace. As you melt in her arms, you feel your creative spirit stirring in your abdomen. Your Mother archetype whispers in your ear, "Bring your creative gifts to the world. Your gifts are uniquely you and others are waiting to be blessed by them." She then blesses you with the ability to give birth to your cherished dreams, and she assures you that she will be there to support you as you nurture and sustain what you give birth to. Your Mother takes a pomegranate from the banquet table and places it in your hand. This is to remind you that you have many seeds inside of you ready to be planted in the world. Plant them with love and grace. You feel the words of your Inner Mother in your womb and you know her presence. You thank her for being there for you, and you know you can call on her at any time.

Your Inner Mother takes your hand and puts it into the hand of your Magical Child, who is dancing with joy to see you and be recognized by you. You kneel down by her and take her into your arms. With a huge smile, she hands you a magic wand and invites you to come play with her in the forest. She tells you there are many magical places you can see together. The magic wand is your gift from her, which blesses you with the ability to imagine many possibilities and to create new meanings from a broken past. You love her excitement and together you dance and sing around the Great Hall. You promise her you will go into the forest after the feast, and that you will never abandon her again. She jumps for joy and takes the hand of your Inner Mother, where she feels safe and warm.

Standing behind your Inner Mother is your Inner Adolescent. You are amazed at how beautiful and calm she is. Along with her beauty, you also see pain and struggle on her face. You slowly walk up to her and she reaches out her hand, which holds the most gorgeous butterfly you have ever seen. She blesses you with the ability to go through painful transitions and emerge transformed. She places the butterfly in your hand, and you watch as the wings unfurl and you sense the freedom to be you. Your Inner Adolescent is always present for you when you need reassurance that you deserve to sometimes go within to find yourself so you can emerge and be free. As you look

into your Inner Adolescent's eyes, your heart connects with hers and
you see butterflies swirling around both of you. Mist fills your eyes
as you thank your Inner Adolescent for being true to herself and for
blessing you with her gifts.

Through the mist in your eyes you see a beautiful, full-bodied
woman reaching out her arms to you. She holds a single pink rose
and brings it to you. As your Inner Lover puts the rose in your hand
she puts her hand on your heart, and you feel the warmth of her
hand on your breasts. Feelings of sexual pleasure begin to stir in
you as she blesses your ability to connect and cherish yourself and
others. She blesses your sexual desire and your ability to use your
femininity to bless and nurture those you love. You feel your heart
open as you take in her blessings, and your senses come alive as you
touch the rose petals, smell the rich aroma, and see the petals of the
rose open, just as you allow your heart to open.

Your eyes work to focus on your next blesser. You can barely see
this woman's form as she comes to you out of the shadows of the
Great Hall. Her face is covered with a veil and she walks cautiously
toward you as you take a step back wondering what blessing she
could possibly bring you. As you stare at her you begin to see a gold
aura around her; underneath her shadowy appearance is a golden
light. She reminds you that Hindus named gold the "mineral light,"
supposing it to come from a mysterious congealment of sunlight
buried underground. Gold is a metaphor for the Divine soul, the
part of you that is incorruptible and changeless. She holds in her
hand a gold ring and invites you to hold out your hand as she puts
the ring on your finger. She blesses you for your willingness to look
at those things in your life you have denied or repressed and to
reclaim the gold that is rightfully yours. This golden part of you is
impervious. It cannot disintegrate or deteriorate. This is the part of
you that will last forever and cannot be destroyed. You thank your

Inner Shadow for her presence and her blessing and for teaching you the value of walking with her so you can find the gold in the dark moments of your life.

You startle as you feel a pressure on your right shoulder, and you turn around to see your Inner Warrior holding a sword in front of your face. She lowers the sword and stands squarely in front of you. You feel her power and strength. She hands you a sword and urges you to use this as a symbol of protection and blessing. She encourages you to set your boundaries and use the sword to protect those boundaries. She blesses you with the strength to take action in your life and to cut through the doubts and fears that keep you stuck. She also hands you a shield to protect your heart when arrows of criticism try to penetrate you. You receive her gifts and her blessing and feel a glow in your solar plexus. You feel your power as a woman and pledge to use her gifts wisely.

You take a deep breath and close your eyes as you let all these blessings flow and mingle in your body. You sense a pair of ancient hands on your shoulders and you open your eyes to see your Inner Crone. In her arms she holds a sky-blue cape covered with sparkling diamonds. She wraps you in the mantle as she blesses you with wisdom to hold all the paradoxes of your life with gentleness. She encourages you not to use this mantle to hide your aging and withdraw from the world, but to wear it with dignity. She blesses you with the gift of accepting your inner knowing and trusting your still, small voice to guide you in all your decisions and actions. She blesses you with the ability to let go of the losses in your life and the things that no longer serve you. You feel the weight of this mantle of blessing, and you know that with your Inner Crone's presence, you can carry this responsibility. She can help you to hold yourself and others with the richness of what she has taught you about life and death. You thank your ancient one, your wise woman, your

Inner Crone for her gift and her blessing.

Silence fills the Great Hall as if time stands still. Then you hear bells ringing in the distance, trumpets playing, signifying time for the coronation of your wholeness as a woman. Your Inner Queen is surrounded by a white light that grows to encompass you in this moment of recognition and achievement. She smiles as pride radiates from her eyes as she slowly removes her crown and slowly places this symbol of completion, honor, and victory on your head. You bow your head and kneel before her to let yourself be honored for what you have accomplished. She blesses you with prosperity, discernment, and confidence. She charges you to step fully into your ability to lead yourself and others. Also, as a Queen, she charges you to let your vision of what is possible for you expand. Now that you are blessed, it is now time for you to bless others so they can become all they are meant to become. You are to go out into your world and share what you have learned about yourself so they can also be whole and prosper.

You take your seat at the round table with all parts of yourself as you celebrate the wholeness of your Woman Within. Your Inner Queen hands you the key to your sacred place and tells you that you have the ability to unlock the door and return here at any time. In fact, she bids you to come here at least once a day to stay in connection with all of who you are. And, especially return when you are confused, unsettled, lonely, afraid, or lost. Also, return when you want to celebrate a victory—or just relish in the richness of who you are. There is no one else like you. You are unique and have a gift to offer others. As Mother Teresa said, "It may be a drop in the ocean, but the ocean would be less without that drop."

Your sacred place lives inside of you every moment of every day. You do not have to go looking for a guru, a saint, priest, or rabbi to find your sacred place. These outside guides can support your journey, yet only you can truly know your uniqueness.

You are precious, irreplaceable. Take time to use your gifts and integrate them into your spirit so you can pass them on to others through service, actions, and your example. Pass on your gifts so others may get to know their sacred place as well.

Blending All the Parts

You are made up of many individual experiences, energies, and unique qualities. Your experiences have created who you are, and each is a piece of the mosaic of your life. It is just as important to step back and view who you are from a distance as it is to look closely at each piece of who you are.

All mosaics need color, shadows, shapes, and different textures to create the masterpiece. Do you spend too much time up close or at a distance? To get the full value of your personal mosaic, study a piece at a time and then step back and see the value of each piece to the whole.

Driving along a country road in Michigan I passed a real estate sign in front of a house. On top of the usual "For Sale" sign was a statement, "I am gorgeous inside." As I drove, I kept repeating that statement over and over. *I am gorgeous inside. I am gorgeous inside.* What makes me gorgeous is knowing all my different archetypes. The shadows and the light pick up the qualities in each of the archetypal energies to form a beautiful me.

The struggle is I don't *feel* gorgeous inside. Some days I feel totally incompetent, clumsy, ugly, deceptive, manipulative, and worthless. I work hard to hide this by smiling, being nice, and lying to myself. It is important that I acknowledge all parts of me and to remember that the key is balance. The key to any artist or decorator is contrast and balance. Look at who you are inside. Take time to shine light on what you *have* done well and step back and look at the wholeness of who you are. You know you are gorgeous inside. As Ralph Waldo Emerson said, "What lies beyond us and what lies before us are tiny matters compared to what lies within us." By going within you will find your unique design. Just as the acorn contains the perfect pattern to become an oak tree, so do you have the perfect pattern to become the magnificent you. You have a built-in system that is guiding and directing you—your archetypes. By becoming conscious of this guidance and by knowing *you* are in charge of each of them, your path to wholeness becomes easier. If you let one or two of your archetypes take over unconsciously, you lose your way. This is when you can return to your sacred place and find what you need to balance your energy within you. You are the creator of your sacred space. Use your power wisely.

About the Author

Charlene Bell Tosi has a bachelor of science degree in nursing from Vanderbilt University; a master of science in educational psychology from University of Wisconsin-Milwaukee; and a certificate in Jungian psychology from the C. J. Jung Institute in Illinois.

Charlene was a public health nurse for five years and a professor of nursing for fifteen years. While at the University of Wisconsin-Milwaukee, she created a successful communication training program for parents and adolescents that was funded by the National Institute for Health and continues to be offered and researched at the University of Wisconsin.

In 1987, Charlene founded the Woman Within Training which continues to be offered to women across the United States, Europe, South Africa, and Australia. She is also the coauthor of several workshops, including Women Empowering Women, Woman Within Level 2, Mother's Shadow, Couples Weekend 1 and 2, and the Sexual Self Workshop.

Charlene maintains a private in-person and phone coaching practice and leads ongoing workshops for couples, men, and women. She lives in Michigan with her husband, Rich Tosi, one of the cofounders of the ManKind project. She is the mother of two sons and the grandmother of four fantastic grandchildren. Visit Charlene's website: www.DiscoverYourWomanWithin.

Sources

Bly, Robert. *A Little Book on the Human Shadow.* New York: Harper Collins, 1988.

Brizendine, Louann. *The Female Brain.* New York: Three Rivers Press, 2007.

Chesler, Phyllis. *Woman's Inhumanity to Woman.* New York: Thunder's Mouth Press/Nation Books, 2001.

Cirlot, J. E. *Dictionary of Symbols.* New York: Philosophical Library, 1991.

Goldsmith, Joel. *Art of Meditation.* New York: Harper and Row, 1956.

Gurian, Michael. *The Wonder of Girls.* New York: Atria Books, 2003.

Johnson, Robert. *Owning Your Own Shadow.* San Francisco: Harper, 1991.

Jones, Don. *Wisdom for the Journey.* Bloomington, IN: AuthorHouse, 2007.

Joseph, Jenny. "When I Am an Old Woman." Minchinhampton, UK: 1961.

Jung, Carl. *Collected Works: Symbols of Transformation.* Princeton, NJ: Princeton University Press, 1977.

Kierkegaard, Søren. *Sickness unto Death.* Radford, VA: Wilder Publications, 2008.

Klein, Josephine. *Our Need for Others and Its Roots in Infancy.* London: Tavistock, 1987.

Miller, Brenda. *Season of the Body.* Louisville, KY: Sarabrande Books, 2002.

Moore, Robert, and Douglas Gillette. *King, Warrior, Magician, and Lover*. San Francisco: Harper Collins, 1990.

Neumann, Erich. *The Great Mother: An Analysis of the Archetype*. Princeton, NJ: Pantheon Books, 1955.

Parry, Danaan. *Warriors of the Heart*. Kalaheo, HI: Earthstewards, 2009.

Smalley, Gary, and John Trent. *The Blessing*. Nashville: Thomas Nelson, 1993.

Tolle, Eckhart. *The Power of Now*. Novato, CA: New World Library, 1999.

Valen, Kelly. *The Twisted Sisterhood*. New York: Ballantine Books, 2010.

Williamson, Marianne. *A Return to Love*. New York: Harper Collins, 1992.

Williamson, Marianne. *A Woman's Worth*. New York: Random House, 1993.

Wiseman, Rosalind. *Queen Bees and Wannabees*. New York: Three Rivers Press, 2002.

Woodman, Marion. *Conscious Femininity*. Toronto: Inner City Books, 1993.

Woodman, Marion. *Dancing in the Flames*. Boston: Shambhala, 1996.

Woodman, Marion. *The Pregnant Virgin*. Toronto: Inner City Books, 1985.

Young-Eisendrath, Polly, and Florence Wiedemann. *Female Authority: Empowering Women through Psychotherapy*. New York: Guilford, 1987

Contributors

Paula Alter lives in England and is a certified facilitator for the Woman Within Trainings. She works in organizational development, focused on dialogue and relationship management. Paula is also a minister who works with clients to create personal and meaningful weddings, baby blessings, and life transition ceremonies. Contact Paula at paula.alter@zen. co.uk.

Kerstin Bandura is an attorney and mother of four children who lives in Bremen, Germany. She is on the facilitation track for the Woman Within Trainings and has staffed Woman Within Level 2. Contact Kerstin at kerstinbardua@aol.com.

Alison Davis lives in France and Switzerland. She is a certified facilitator for the Woman Within Trainings. She is a coach who works with teenagers, couples, and senior business executives. Alison excels at inspiring others to create work-life balance, live happier lives, and achieve their full potential. Contact Alison at alisondaviscoaching.com.

Kathy Entrup, MS, LCP, LCPC, is a psychotherapist who lives in Quincy, Illinois. She specializes in the treatment and prevention of trauma and is certified in EMDR. Kathy is dedicated to empowering young girls through the creation of the Girls Rock Program. Contact Kathy at kentrup@gmail.com

Rhonda Gaughan, MA, is from Louisiana and is a certified weekend leader for Woman Within Trainings. She created The Art of Your Soul, a workshop designed to explore and express creativity. Rhonda and her husband John facilitate workshops designed to inspire couples to reach deeper levels of love, intimacy, and trust. Contact Rhonda at www.TrueNsight.com.

Lisa Hines attended the Women Within Training inspired by her longtime interest in Jungian psychology and the work of Marion Woodman. She is a single mother raising four teenage boys. Lisa is the owner of Stage to Show, the largest home-staging company on the East Coast. Contact Lisa at www.StageToShow.com.

Judith Pauly lives in San Diego, California, and is a certified facilitator for Woman Within, serving the organization in many capacities for more than twenty years. She incorporates NLP, Pranic Healing, Landmark Education, and religious studies in her work. In her seventies, Judith travels around the world leading workshops and sharing her wisdom. Contact Judith at www.PaulySoulStuff.com.

Amy Pershing lives in Ann Arbor, Michigan, and is the clinical director of the Center for Eating Disorders in Ann Arbor, as well as owner of Pershing Turner Center in Annapolis, Maryland. She cofounded the Binge Eating Disorder Association and is the president-elect. Amy developed the Bodywise program for clients with binge-eating disorders and Hungerwise to provide recovery from chronic dieting and weight cycling. Contact Amy at www.HungerWise.com.

Monica Robinson, MSW, LCSW, lives in Chicago and is a certified weekend leader for Woman Within Trainings and a co-creator of Woman Within Level 2. Specializing in the areas of life transitions, trauma, grief and loss, depression and anxiety, Monica believes that creating a human life is as much walking through mud as it is dancing in the light. Contact Monica at monicarobin@sbcglobal.net.

Page Rossiter lives in Abu Dhabi, UAE, is a certified facilitator for Woman Within Trainings and facilitator for the Empowered Girls Alliance. For more than ten years, Page has led women's circles, which create authentic community. She holds a degree in business administration and developed her powerful coaching skills with the

International Coaching Society and Coaches Training Institute. Contact Page at RealPage@gmail.com.

Marcia Stone lives in Indianapolis, Indiana, and is a certified facilitator for Woman Within Trainings. For more than thirty years Marcia has worked in advertising design as a creative person. She now has dual roles as a design practitioner and teacher in Visual Communication and as author of *The Creative Director Survival Guide*.

Lynn Trotta is a facilitator in training for Woman Within Trainings. Since 2002 Lynn has facilitated nature-based programs to connect participants to the wisdom of the natural world and to their own true nature. As a life coach, she helps pregnant women prepare for motherhood and supports all women to release their pasts so they may move forward. Lynn lives in New York and can be reached at trottacoaching@gmail.com.

Acknowledgments

To the thousands of women who have participated in the Woman Within Trainings: Thank you for trusting the process and teaching me so much!

To the hundreds of women who have participated in Woman Within Level 2: Archetypes of the Castle: Thank you for encouraging me to write a book so you could read more about the archetypes of women.

To my husband: Thank you for your encouragement through the years as you have watched me put this book on the shelf and then take it off again time after time. Your faith and belief it me has truly been the wind beneath my wings.

To my sons: Thank you for giving me the experience of being a mother. You have gifted me with so much happiness. A special thanks to my son Tony for designing my book cover and website, and a special thanks to my son David for keeping me in tune with all the technological changes.

To my mother and dad: Thank you for giving me life and teaching me so many important lessons—and for blessing me!

To my sisters and brother: Thank you for all the ways you have stood by me through the many paths that I have taken as I discovered my Woman Within.

To Patricia Clason: Thank you for inspiring me to do personal growth work and for being the catalyst to begin my healing journey.

To the ManKind Project: Thank you for blazing the trail for the empowerment of men and for being an inspiration for many women to attend the Woman Within Training.

To the many women who helped and facilitated the creation of the Woman Within Training: Susan Ballje, Nan Luedtke, Ro Getto, Chris Waters, Kathy Porter, and Michelle Conlin were the original group who birthed the program, and later Kenna del Sol, Doris Couch, Julie Berg-Einhorn, Judith Pauly, and many others added their wisdom to the program—Thank you for your creative spirit!

To the many women who nursed Woman Within through many changes by serving on the advisory council, the board, and administering and breathing life into it through the past twenty-five years: Thank you for keeping the vision alive and thriving through your years of service.

To my dear friend and the keeper of the heart of Woman Within: Margaret Renaud, executive administrator, whose tireless work continues to keep the flame of this organization bright and burning!

To the women who serve the regions of Woman Within International: Thank you for your loyal energy to deliver the program through your diligence, volunteerism, and dedication to the healing of women.

To the past and present Weekend Leaders of the Woman Within Training: Thank you for taking on the leadership role to oversee the program in a safe, meaningful way.

To the leaders of Woman Within Level 2: Thank you Monica Robinson and Esther Robertson for your creativity and perseverance to develop and deliver such a meaningful, dynamic program.

To the facilitators and facilitators in training: Thank you for giving of your time and talents so women can have a place to heal.

To my present Empowerment Circle: Thank you, Amy Pershing, Maria McEvoy, Jenny Knopf, and Terri Wilkerson, for encouraging me when I wanted to give up and for believing in me.

To the thousands of men who have participated in the Mother's Shadow workshop: Thank you for teaching me about the power of the Mother archetype.

To the thousands of couples who have participated in the Couples Weekend: Thank you for teaching me about how the archetypal energy affects relationships.

To the two people who kept my body relaxed and balanced: Thank you Tom and Susan Hauer for your beautiful healing talents!

To my mentors and inspirers: Thank you, Marion Woodman, Diane Martin, Robert Moore, Djohariah Toor, Judith Duerk, Karen Kahn, Naomi Davis, Dennis Ondrejka, Mary Mundt, and Kathie Wickstrand, for believing in me and inspiring me to be an author.

To my book coach: Thank you, Patricia Lynn Reilly, for holding me through this process and teaching me how to be an author so I could finally give birth to this book.

To my manuscript readers: Thank you Renée Riley-Adams, Jenny Sheets, Christine Tosi, Terri Wilkerson, Maria McEvoy, Jim McEvoy, Tracey Sheely, Ro Getto, Nan Luedtke, James Adams, and Amy Pershing, for taking the time to read parts of my manuscript and cheer me on!

To my editor: Thank you Pam Suwinsky for your encouragement and your brilliance for seeing and guiding me in creating the final product.

About the Woman Within Training

The Woman Within Training is an experiential, residential weekend training for women who want to discover the power of who they are. At this training women have the opportunity to explore many areas of their lives through visualizations, journaling, small group work, and individual work. The training is offered in many areas of the United States, Europe, South Africa, and Australia. To find out more about the Woman Within Training, visit the website: www. WomanWithin.org

Participants' Praise for the Woman Within Training
"Trainers dealt with some incredible issues. The women on the course were brave and it is fantastic to be witness and share in their transition. Trainers/organizers of this are brilliant."

"I feel happier and more confident to be the woman I am, with many tools to remind me when I forget."

"I found it incredible and one of the most amazing experiences of my life."

"This training has given me strength and direction. I mentor teenage girls and I feel inspired to support that work."

"It will benefit me every day as I have reconnected with my ability to set limits, connect with my anger and be able to make changes in my life instead of taking life as it comes."

"I have released grief from my past and reclaimed parts of myself that were shut down."

"I reconnected with my womanhood, what it means to be a woman and my courage. This will benefit me and all the women I love as I can share that beauty with them."

"Helped me break free from damaging beliefs and connect with my true self. I can now hear my inner self."

"I have reclaimed two aspects of myself that were chained and locked away—my hellion she-bear and my neglected beautiful self. Both are now part of me."

"I can now breathe into all my parts and love my whole self."

About the Woman Within Level 2: Archetypes of the Castle

Woman Within Level 2 is five-day program that examines in depth the nine feminine archetypes. It is led and taught by certified leaders and facilitators of the Woman Within Training. After a dynamic presentation of each archetypal energy, women are facilitated through a process to ground and free up this energy in their bodies. The Woman Within Training, described on page 227, is a prerequisite for attending this program. To find out more, visit the website: www.WomanWithin.org

Participants' Praise for Woman Within Level 2
"It helped me give a name to all of the different aspects of myself. Helped to provide clarity, everything is not just one big messy soup. We have control over the ingredients and seasonings!"

"I was able to connect and identify many parts of myself. I had no idea I was capable of going so deep in so many levels and various archetypes at once. AMAZING! The information for my mind on what my behavior means is invaluable; the experience for my body of working through my deepest archetypes is unforgettable."

"Fantastic workshop. I am very glad I attended. This workshop helped me to discover my Queen, my magnificence, my vulnerability and more. Thanks a lot!!!"

"I really felt a shift after Level 1, but Level 2 touched my soul in a way I have only dreamt of. My body will never forget what it was like to *finally* know how to release my warrior energy and to do it in a safe place."

"Multiple processes moved energy regularly and now I can say that I get it. I fully understand that I am perfectly suited for every aspect of my life and mission and that I can write the story of my life."

"I was able to really look at the different archetypes in my life and essentially rewrite the story of my life. I feel so fortunate to be able to delve deeply into myself at such a young age and reexamine my own archetypes of stories. I love it!"

"I rediscovered long-forgotten parts of myself and found new aspects of myself by watching others. It reminded me that I have value, worth, and something uniquely significant to give to the world."

"I found the archetypes really useful in identifying the various parts of my jigsaw. Both the performance lectures and the processes were useful to help me get to know the archetypes in me and to allow me to learn more about myself."

"I could access my different archetypes—found my warrior again, which I had forgotten, and reclaimed my lover energy. Now I feel I can notice which archetype is running when I am in crisis, and have the choice to bring in a different archetype to help."

"Studying the archetypes and processing them through experiential work has been incredible from a personal growth perspective. I love understanding these different energies and they've unblocked parts of me which have felt 'stuck' for years."

"It really clarified the archetype model and where on each spectrum I sit. A really powerful tool to self-knowledge and understanding. It is clear that acceptance and connection are the keys for me."

"The workshop has brought a tremendous amount of awareness to the way I live my life and see the world. I have learned from doing and being and observing, sensing during all the lectures and processes."

"The presentations were FANTASTIC; professional, funny, excellent personal testimonies. To then embed the theory through a process was perfect."